HELP!

Survival strategies for teachers

Kathy Paterson

Pembroke Publishers Limited

© 1993 Pembroke Publishers Limited
538 Hood Road
Markham, Ontario L3R 3K9

Canadian Cataloguing in Publication Data

Paterson, Kathleen M.,
  Help!: survival strategies for teachers

ISBN 1-55138-002-1

1. Teachers. 2. Teaching. I. Title.

LB1025.3.P38 1993   371.1'.02   C93-093313-3

Editor: Kate Revington
Design: John Zehethofer
Cover Photography: Ajay Photographics
Typesetting: Jay Tee Graphics Ltd.

Printed and bound in Canada
9 8 7 6 5 4 3 2 1

Contents

Introduction

For a person to be a truly effective teacher, he or she must embody two great loves: a love of learning and a love of children. Having met these most important prerequisites, the prospective teacher must satisfy standards of achievement in areas of theory and curriculum, and upon graduation be ready to teach successfully. Teaching, however, encompasses so much more than a knowledge of child development, reading and math curricula, teaching techniques, evaluation procedures and so on. Consider the many diverse roles a teacher must play: artist, interior decorator, nurse, doctor, counsellor, author, accountant, secretary, concert director, playwright, scientist, coach, detective, police officer, referee, matchmaker, technician, entertainer, parent and parent adviser, reporter, psychologist and, most recently, fund raiser. None of these other roles are genuine teaching roles; however, because such parts are so often played by teachers, it is on these or at least some of them that this book focuses.

My intention is to provide ideas that will assist both beginning teachers and experienced teachers looking for reinforcement to fulfill their many duties beyond the teaching of curriculum. The suggestions represent original thoughts and ideas, plus, I believe, unique translations of what I have experienced and learned from peers over 15 years of teaching. I hope all these suggestions constitute a valuable compendium for teachers.

I hope, too, that this manual will make the multifaceted nature of the teaching profession seem less formidable by providing readily accessible, practical, hands-on ideas. For, in the words of Thomas Huxley, "The great end of life is not knowledge, but action."

The first edition of *Help!*, called *for teachers* (1986), was designed primarily for elementary school teachers. Although many of the ideas work equally well at any grade level, including high school, this edition makes special reference to Junior High school. In addition, it includes a chapter on the special students who are being integrated into regular classrooms (see Chapter 7, **Coping**).

Sometimes, people who are not teachers think teaching is easy. We know better! *Help! Survival Strategies for Teachers* is dedicated to teachers who want to teach boldly, and who know that in order to accomplish great things, they must not only act, but must also dream; must not only plan, but must also believe.

Acknowledgment

Special thanks to Dr. Fern Snart, friend and adviser, for her unwavering support and confidence in me; to Erin, for her youthful input; and to my husband, Gerry, for his inexhaustible wealth of knowledge.

CHAPTER 1

Motivating

This book begins with a chapter on motivating, because, as every teacher knows, unmotivated students do not learn, and the teacher's job becomes much harder. Each year, it seems, students come to school with less intrinsic motivation than the year before. Rather than attempting to explain this phenomenon, or justify lazy teaching techniques because of it, the teacher needs to assume a positive attitude and to face the lack-of-motivation dilemma head-on. If you can motivate your students, then you will have taken the first step toward creating the right attitude for learning!

A. Getting Off to a Good Start

> I swear I merely blinked an eye,
> And summer left with no goodbye,
> Now all these duties must be met —
> Help me! I'm not quite ready yet!
> — *K. Paterson*

Even the most experienced teacher may face the first day of the school year with considerable anxiety. Not knowing the students and their capabilities and having few or no supplies, together with the shock of returning to that confined space filled with a sea of either excited, expectant faces or defiant, impassive ones (as you may have in Junior High), can lead to a day of disorganized disaster! But Day One should be an exciting, well-planned day which sets the classroom atmosphere for the rest of the year and leaves the students eagerly anticipating what is to come.

Given the general confusion affecting that first day — and week — I admit that generating excitement for the school year is difficult, but doing so is not impossible. Here are some suggestions of things to do in addition to the duties you are required to do, taking attendance, passing out supplies, and showing the location of fire exits being among them.

- Instead of having students write or discuss what they did that summer, have them describe a situation in which they may or may not have participated during the summer. Perhaps they could write first, then work in small groups. The listeners must try to guess the validity of the speaker's story or various parts of it. Exaggeration is encouraged. Be sure to tell a model story first.
- Start the day by talking about yourself — your experiences, hobbies, pets — anything that might be of interest to your students. You will become more real to them and a rapport can begin to develop.
- Early in the first week (possibly as soon as the afternoon of Day One), have a seat switch, where one or two students leave the room, and while they are out, two others switch seats. The object is for the first two to discover who has changed places. Doing so is challenging; names, as well as locations, must be recalled. (CAUTION: Ask for volunteers to leave the room. A self-conscious or shy child might be mortified if put in the position of not knowing names, etc., so early in the year. Students who volunteer to go out are generally the ones whose confidence can handle such a situation.)
- Ask each student to make an original sign, nameplate or poster to attach to the front of his/her desk. Provide the necessary paper, crayons, and so on.
- Have a group discussion about possible field trips, excursions and extra-curricular activities, drawing out general areas of group interest, and voting to ascertain specific places. (You will gain insights into your students, and they will become excited about future events.)
- At the Junior High level, you can talk about specific special events students might like to see occur, such as dances, hot dog days, and color days.
- Bring a toy or souvenir that has something to do with your summer and use it as a discussion opener. If you didn't do anything exciting over the summer, think back over earlier holidays to find something appealing.
- Discover their music. Surprise Junior High students by bringing

a poster of a popular musical group or star. Know the name(s) as well as some interesting trivia. (Get help from any local music store.) You never know, you might come to like the group!

- Explain to younger students exactly what they can expect in the way of exciting curriculum; for example, "We will learn how pioneers made butter. Maybe we'll try churning it ourselves."
- Hand out brief outlines of each subject, and highlight points that may be of particular interest to your students. For example: "Science: Ecosystems...field trip to a swamp to collect frog eggs..." Students will then know what to look forward to, and if you are excited, then they will be too!
- Invite older students to write (print) a paragraph, a list, or a story telling about their favorite subject — themselves! First, show something you've written about yourself as a model. Then, give a specific length of time — usually 10 to 15 min is enough. Be sure to tell students that you will not be marking their work. Collect the assignments, allowing students to share if they want to, and save them until the following June, when the same assignment will be given. Then you can compare the two pieces for growth and development. Asking younger students to draw pictures of themselves has the same merits.
- Present several books that you have chosen to read to the class. Read and discuss the synopsis of each and have the class vote on the book to be read. Then begin reading the book immediately. Even Junior High students love being read to.
- Have available one copy or sample of each of the texts to be used that year. Introduce each one, giving your own reasons for liking it. If you do not particularly like part of a text, be honest about it, but be sure students realize they are hearing only your opinions. (Students have a right to know why specific texts are being used, and sharing this information with them helps in the establishment of rapport.)
- Discuss your expectations and ask for theirs as well. Follow up by summarizing, in list form, teacher's rights, students' rights and a few class rules on which everyone agrees.

The following lists of teacher and student rights reflect both Elementary and Junior High student input and have been compiled by the author. They should be used as starting points only; it is important that each class formulate its own lists. (Note that points 2 to 8 under "Teacher's Rights" all expand upon the first theme of respect.)

TEACHER'S RIGHTS

1. To be treated with respect by the students.
2. To be allowed to talk without interruption.
3. To expect that homework will be done (unless there are extenuating circumstances).
4. To be allowed to make mistakes and be human.
5. To show emotion such as anger or excitement when appropriate.
6. To sometimes have "bad days" when he or she has less patience, etc.
7. To never be sworn at or hit by students.
8. To have a private space, such as the desk, or special drawer, where students are not allowed to put or remove items at any time.

STUDENTS' RIGHTS

1. To be respected by the teacher.
2. To expect that the teacher is honest and trustworthy.
3. To feel confident that the teacher will not embarrass any student in any way.
4. To be allowed to work without interruption from peers.
5. To be judged fairly; teachers should not have pets or show favoritism.
6. To be allowed to make mistakes without feeling stupid.
7. To be encouraged, but not forced to do something that the student finds very difficult, for example, giving an oral report.
8. To be treated as individuals; all students are different.
9. To have a private space for personal belongings.
10. To have the teacher prepared to teach, not just "winging it."
11. To make decisions about at least some of the assignments; to be given choices.
12. To be treated as young people, not like babies.

- Bring a trinket for each student as a "welcome to this room" token. Trinkets need not be costly (teachers are notoriously broke in September); their value is in the positive feeling they help create. Examples of such trinkets are erasers, special pencils, party toys, balloons (great if they can be printed with your room number), special pens, even large stickers such as you can buy at most card stores. In a pinch, "edibles" will even work. And if you are really energetic, make cookies or brownies.

  NOTE: Don't overlook this idea at Junior High! It may be even more effective there than in elementary school where the students tend to be motivated already. Stickers from local music stores or buttons with sayings such as "Party Animal" are other trinket ideas.

- Place a large piece of paper (at least 1 m sq) on the board or wall and have each student sign it with colored felts. Older students can be encouraged to add such sayings as "Have a happy day." The paper can then be mounted on your door or bulletin board with a "Welcome to Room ____" heading.

- Have each student draw a self-portrait in humorous or cartoon fashion, exaggerating one or two of his/her most obvious features or talents; for example, a young hockey player could be holding a huge hockey stick. Keep it "funny," so that less artistic students do not feel awkward. Provide a model, a picture you've done of yourself. For those students who simply can't get started, offer silhouette outlines (contour drawings sans features) of heads, to which they can add details. Then all the pictures can be mounted collage fashion and labelled "Our Class." (You will find this activity a great icebreaker.)

- Discuss the Physical Education program for the upcoming year. Make particular mention of team sports, intramurals, and extracurricular activities which are so important at the Junior High level. Most students love the gym, but keep an open eye for those few whose faces will show concern at this time, and be prepared to offer alternatives or counselling later. Ask students what games, activities, and specific sports they like best. Students should realize that their preferences *will* be given consideration, so don't say you will give it unless you mean it.

- You can also lead into an informal discussion about current popular teams and players. Ask a few leading questions, for example, Is your favorite basketball player Michael Jordan?

Just be sure to know some facts so that you can begin or carry on the discussion. Usually, Junior High students love to talk on these issues, and having them do so fosters a warmer atmosphere.

- Make ID cards for each student ahead of time, and hand them out on Day One. Make a master, photocopy it, fill in students' names, add stickers or stamps if you have any, and laminate. Students will probably lose their cards, but they do love them. Here is an example.

GRADE 4 STUDENT

Room 6
Teacher: Mrs. Smith
Hillcrest School
1992-93

More than anything else, remember to be enthusiastic and excited about the upcoming year, and to send students home with at least some general ideas of what to expect. In my opinion, you should not begin formal teaching on this first, so very important, day. Day One is a day for getting acquainted and for setting a positive tone. Be creative, and begin a year of learning together, for as every teacher knows, "To teach is to learn again." And smile! For truly, as Dian Ritter writes in *Ginger Snaps: Fun Thoughts on Life*, "Your day (and your year) will go the way the corners of your mouth turn!"

B. Getting To Know Your Students

> Children in a class are like flowers in a bouquet:
> There's always one determined to face the wrong
> way, one that wilts before the rest, one that looks
> more radiant than the entire bunch.
>
> — *Oscar Wilde*

Teachers usually spend more time per day with their students than do the parents of those students, yet frequently don't ever truly get to know those children. This reality is particularly true in secondary school, when teachers are faced with hundreds of different adolescents daily, most of whom don't even know themselves! In either case, understanding the academic, athletic or artistic abilities of their students is not enough. A good teacher assumes the responsibility of getting to know the *whole* child — the person who exists outside school hours — as a total human being, not just a body in a classroom. For only in this way can he or she create the meaningful and motivating learning situations that will help each individual student to develop and grow.

Students need appropriate stimuli. For example, giving an artistic, introverted young man who dislikes contact sports a story to read about wrestling may very well be a complete waste of time. If the teacher wants to create a positive classroom atmosphere where students want to learn, then that teacher must get to know those students.

How does a teacher accomplish this? There are some students whom the teacher may never really know or understand, (or, horrors, even *like*), but, by and large, most students are willing, and even happy, to share their lives with so significant an adult as The Teacher! If The Teacher is genuinely interested, students will reveal more of themselves and, before long, be recognizable as people with a wide variety of interests, abilities, fears, hopes and so on.

However, remember that children have an uncanny ability to detect when adults are superficial in their interest and will react accordingly. Concern must be genuine, or not expressed at all. But, as a human, you can't be expected to remember everything about everyone. Children are incredibly forgiving as long as they know you are forthright and honest in your dealings with them.

There are many ways to get to know your students. The ideas that follow have proved effective in both elementary and Junior High grades. When perusing them, though, bear in mind that unless a suggestion feels right for you, don't use it.

- Begin the year by letting students choose where to sit. Make it clear that they must choose a seat where they can expect to get their work done and that only you can change an arrangement, something for which two warnings would be given first. On "Choice Day," allow 15 min for students to get their preferred seats. Much bribery and negotiation will take place. And what you will have is an instant sociogram. You can readily

15

identify loners, most popular students, etc.
- Have students complete checklists of descriptive words, indicating which words describe themselves. Assure them that responses will be kept confidential, and that there are no right or wrong answers. If students trust you, this exercise can be quite revealing; children tend to be very honest about themselves, but if you get different responses to similar ideas, take note. I have found it useful to save these lists and have the same forms, which I draw up myself, completed again later in the year for comparison. (See the All About You checklist below, and note the deliberate inclusion of similar ideas.)

ALL ABOUT YOU

Name _____

Write either YES or NO beside each word or phrase. If you think the item says something about you, write YES. If you think it does not describe you, write NO. If you are unsure about it, put nothing, but try to leave few blanks.

1. Honest_____
2. Attractive_____
3. Friendly_____
4. Hardworking_____
5. Athletic_____
6. Good weight_____
7. Happy_____
8. Physically strong_____
9. Well-liked_____
10. Like school_____

11. Dependable_____
12. Popular_____
13. Good-looking_____
14. Smart_____
15. Well-dressed_____
16. Generous_____
17. Healthy_____
18. Am a good friend_____
19. Am a good student_____
20. Like myself_____

- Ask for several students to assist you with after-school tasks (e.g., duplicating, cleaning the room, preparing art projects, even marking). Although you may very well be able to do the work faster yourself, consider how much you can learn from and about your students during these more informal times.
- Ask older students to create autobiographies. Be sure to point out that you are interested in the substance of what they say,

not their writing skills. They can accomplish this task by cartooning; writing a character analysis; writing "The Story of My Life"; making a "Me" poster; or creating "lists" about themselves. Have a few autobiographies of yourself to motivate your students and model for them.

- Eat lunch together as a class. Order a pizza; bring bag lunches; have a sandwich potluck; share a "Witches' Brew Soup," where everyone brings a can of soup and you mix them all together; or try an old-fashioned Box Social. (See "Class Parties," pages 92-93.)

- Take a few students at a time out for lunch at a fast food place. You may not even have to pay; students, if they can, often wish to treat the teacher. Organize the activity, telling all students they will have a turn, and give it your time. A little of your time spent in getting to know your students and winning them over goes a long way toward making your job more pleasurable and profitable.

- Show and Tell is well known, but you can introduce a Sharing Myself time as well. Students, on a rotating basis, share something of importance that has happened to them. Be sure that you participate actively, too.

- A suggestion box in your room can provide insights into what students feel is important. All suggestions must be signed in order to be given consideration, and, of course, they will be kept confidential unless the student requests otherwise. A simple way to enable younger children who can't put thoughts on paper well to participate is to match them with children in an older grade for a 15-min period every so often. The older buddies serve as scribes for the younger students. (I'm sure you can see many additional benefits from this exercise.)

- At the Junior High level, you might label a box "Compliments and Complaints." Plan to share some of the compliments and deal with some of the complaints on a one-to-one basis.

- Have a baby picture board, where each student's baby picture is mounted. If names are omitted, a great guessing game can develop. For the few students who can't come up with a baby picture, you can, together, draw a comical picture or cut one from a magazine. (Enjoying a board of teacher baby pictures can also be a great rapport builder.)

- Be prepared to visit each student at least once during the term at some after-school activity in which he or she participates.

You might attend a dance review, piano recital, Cub or Brownie meeting, band concert, hockey or soccer game. If you're lucky, several students will be on the same team, so one visit to a game allows you to watch them all at once. This scenario is often the case in Junior High and every teacher should attend games at least occasionally anyways. Virtually nothing makes a student prouder than to have his or her teacher at one of these events, and your presence gives you, the teacher, a whole new insight into the student. You may think that you are far too busy with planning and marking for such frivolities, but the time will be well spent.

- Establish a routine of individual interviews. Every couple of weeks, or even monthly, arrange a time when each student meets with you privately, perhaps in a corner of the classroom or just outside the classroom door. Both you and the student can present beefs and bouquets and talk about things that are going well and areas of concern. While you talk, the rest of the class does individual work.

    Trust is important; the student must know that what is said will be kept in confidence. (If you find yourself getting into something that you don't feel you can keep in confidence, tell the student immediately and allow him or her to choose whether or not to continue.)

    When students leave their interviews, be sure they have received something that will make them feel good, a warm fuzzy as Joan Pickart, author of *Warm Fuzzies*, would say: a hug might be enough but giving something tangible, such as a gift of stickers, is often desirable. (See "Teacher-Supplied Treats.") Also, students should leave an interview having a goal or technique on which to concentrate between then and the next meeting. Between interviews, keep a little book up-to-date with relevant points.

    NOTE: These individual interviews become so important to students that they get very upset if anything interferes with their predetermined discussion time. Even the youngest students and the most hardened adolescents look forward to this time alone with the teacher, and the teacher, in turn, learns much about the students.

- If your students already maintain journals, or "daily logs," every once in a while have them evaluate something they have

TEACHER-SUPPLIED TREATS

Obviously, a compliment, a smile, a pat on the head, a wink and such are the best forms of reinforcement to use. However, what if these aren't enough? What if the student doesn't care what you think, and no amount of social reinforcement is going to motivate him or her? Then it is time for other types of reinforcement, always given with social reinforcement, of course. Here are some examples:

1. School Items: erasers, pens, pencils, boxes of paper clips (amazingly popular), note pads....
2. Novelty Items: silly pencils, stamps, stickers, "junk" from flea markets, collected items (such as seashells)
3. Edibles: anything from raisins to peanuts, to chocolate chips, pretzels, jube jubes, and wrapped candies
4. Teacher Time: Give the student a set amount of your time for one-on-one tutoring, talking, game playing, walking, whatever. One-on-one basketball was a favorite with Junior High students, because I always lost!
5. Free Time: ten minutes of absolutely free time...taken when appropriate.
6. Birthday Favors: These are inexpensive and fun. Little items such as balloons and whistles work well with younger children. Junior High students like balloons too.
7. Fortune Cookies: There is something magical about these inexpensive treats!

attempted, either failed or accomplished, being sure to model the skill of self-evaluation first. (See the Goal Setting form on page 27.)

Ask students' permission to read their journals and self-evaluations and you'll learn a lot about their concerns, self-concepts and self-expectations.

• Make a huge people chart! On a large chart, the bigger the better, put every student's name and at least one interesting piece of information about him/her: for example, Name, Birthday, Pet Peeve, Favorite Color, Favorite TV Show or Rock Star. You might have a mini-paragraph after each name.

I have successfully used a circle where the centre said, "Our Colorful Class," and each name and bits of information radiated out from the centre like the spokes of a wheel. Not only do students *love* seeing something about themselves up on the wall so affirmatively, but a chart such as this will constantly remind you of the uniqueness of each of your students.

- Early in the year, go on several field trips, where the sole intent is for you and your students to mingle and enjoy one another's company. (Only when they are away from school confines do the true personalities surface!) Examples of fun trips are hikes (even just around the neighborhood), tobogganing, skating, rollerblading, visiting a senior citizens' home (loved by the residents too!), going for a picnic, or taking a trip to a zoo or pool.

- Consider playing video games. I found that a half-hour trip to a nearby arcade was a huge success with Junior High students. We collected a bit of money through a bottle drive first, so that each student had the same number of quarters. Then we spent a super 30 min in an arcade. Doing this may seem like a radical move, but with Junior High students, "radical" is often the only way to establish rapport!

- Make a photo display. Each student mounts a self-photo and writes a description to go with it. (Younger children can use parents or older buddies as scribes.) Leave the display in a special area of the room. Not only will students be drawn to it continually; but you, as the silent observer, will learn bits and pieces about how they view themselves and others. Be sure to add a photo of yourself, the sillier the better, to the display.

   NOTE: It might be wise to have a camera available for "snapping" those few children who do not have pictures of themselves.

- Write a brief story about the escapades of the whole class. Be creative! Imagine them stranded on a deserted island, lost in a jungle, captured by pirates, crashed at the South Pole, lost in space or even captured in some magical fantasy. If you are sure you can't create such a story, "borrow" an already written one and simply use all the children's names throughout it. Or, you can make the creation of the story a class project (whole writing approach) or a group project. Children *love* to read about themselves (immature egotism is a wonderful tool to utilize in establishing rapport). And if you use the students themselves to give you the story ideas, many interesting facts arise as to how they view themselves and others in such a setting. For example, who will be the leaders? the doctors? the workers?

NOTE: Junior High students may wish to write these stories with partners or even individually. Allowing them to do so can be useful because you can see when students view themselves differently from the way in which they are seen by peers. All the information gleaned will help you to get to know the "whole" child.

- Ask students to draw cartoons of themselves in which areas of strength are exaggerated and areas of weakness minimized. You will, of course, have to do a model cartoon of yourself. You can also show Junior High students political cartoons on an overhead projector for inspiration.
- Have students complete open-ended sentence questionnaires. Students are usually quite happy to fill these in, and will, as a rule, be truthful. These can be a valuable source of information for the teacher who can, of course, structure the sentences in any way desired. See "Getting To Know You — A Questionnaire" on page 22.

With very young children, you may have to use the older buddy system, or complete the lists during one-on-one chats. I have found that students generally complete these questionnaires openly and honestly, as long as they know that the answers will be kept confidential. Those students who do *not* answer honestly are readily obvious, and this, too, provides the teacher with valuable information about them.

> In the end, the mind of the teacher is the most
> powerful influence in any classroom. What she knows
> and believes about children will create the
> atmosphere affecting their learning.
>
> — *Alice Yardley*

GETTING TO KNOW YOU — A QUESTIONNAIRE

Name _____

Complete each sentence with your first reactions. Be honest!

1. I get angry when _____

2. What I like best about school is _____

3. I am proud of myself when _____

4. I feel lonely when _____

5. My favorite out-of-school activity is _____

6. The thing in life most important to me is _____

7. My best friend(s) is/are _____

8. School would be better if _____

9. Most of the time I am _____

10. The thing I hate most about school is _____

11. My parents are _____

12. I worry about _____

13. The thing I like best about myself is _____

14. If I could change one thing about myself it would be _____

_____

15. At school I have a lot of trouble with _____

16. My favorite TV show is _____

17. My favorite kind of book or story is _____

18. I like a teacher to be _____

19. I would like to be better at _____

20. One thing that scares me is _____

CHAPTER 2

Guiding

The critical role of guiding, or counselling, students is readily delegated to teachers with the irrational assumption that they (we) have somehow, magically, incorporated all the knowledge and skills necessary to master this task. This is not so! To my knowledge, no course is offered on student counselling per se. Of course, if the teacher-to-be has been fortunate enough to have taken a psychology course or two, he or she *may* have acquired a few counselling skills, but that is uncommon. Nevertheless, one does not learn how to deal with the multitude of problems, concerns, frustrations, anxieties and fears presented by students until facing them daily. There are, therefore, no hard and fast rules about guiding students; however, keep in mind two concepts that are significant to and have unmeasurable importance in any counselling scenario: honesty and empathy.

A. Developing Positive Self-Concepts

> A child brings his self-concept with him — he doesn't park it at the door; whatever we do affects his self-concept, even when we are teaching him mathematics, languages, or how to roller skate.
> — *Arthur W. Combs*

Teachers today are constantly being challenged to consider the child's self-concept, and almost every book on teaching offers suggestions about how this can be done. I believe that good teachers innately assist their students to feel better about themselves, and don't, therefore, need constant reminding of the many common-sense approaches to this problem. Therefore, in this section, I will try to offer a few original ideas, with which even the best teachers may not already be familiar.

First, however, a word of caution. Children are unique, and so, what works with one, or even with the majority, may not work with another. An amusing epigram states that "some people are so sensitive they feel snubbed if an epidemic overlooks them." Humorous as it is, this statement appears to be true of some children whose apparently exaggerated sensitivity makes the choice of self-confidence building techniques problematic. Before implementing any new idea intended to foster the growth of positive self-concepts — know your students! Make sure you don't embarrass or put down one student in an attempt to build up another. If Johnnie is quite sensitive, although smart, and you say, "Good for you, Sam! You beat Johnnie on this test," you may do a lot more harm to Johnnie than good to Sam. Comparisons such as this should never be made — the risk of emotional injury to a child is too great — yet teachers unintentionally fall into the habit.

Here are a few possibly different and useful techniques for building confidence.

- Estabish a Be-Nice-to... week. Students' names are drawn randomly to select the "student of the week." That person's name is written with washable felt marker on a large "Be nice to —" laminated poster for the duration of the week. During that week, this student is allowed little desirable privileges which may include being first in line, assisting the teacher, and being dismissed early for lunch.

  In addition, the other students are encouraged to be extra nice to the designated student. (I must admit that this idea works much better with younger children who are more easily influenced, but you could still try it at the Junior High level.)

  On the last day of that week, each student anonymously writes out a few things they admire or like about the selected student. But before they first do this, brainstorm for a long list of "describers"; otherwise, students fall readily into the "I like him. He is nice" trap.

  Finally, compile the list, type it up, (adding a few statements where necessary), and present the letter, in an official sealed envelope, to the student. Students can hardly wait to receive their letter, and many mothers have told me that these special documents remained affixed to fridges for a very long time.

- Read or tell the story in *Warm Fuzzies* by Joan Pickart (1988) to your class, then periodically take a few moments to give warm fuzzies to students. Encourage students to participate in warm fuzzy sharing too, but help them to be specific about why they are doing it. For example: "I want to give a warm fuzzy to Billy because he let me use his new crayons." Of course, what you are really doing is encouraging them to express gratitude or appreciation.

NOTE: As any type of positive reinforcement can be used manipulatively, be aware of this possibility and step in, if needed. I have not, however, encountered this problem because students seem to enjoy the giving process.

Also encourage students to recognize anyone who looks like he or she could use a boost. Children become amazingly profifient at doing this in a very short time.

- Pass a Hug is a very similar to the giving of warm fuzzies, except that the children sit in a circle (or two or three circles depending on numbers) on the floor and hold hands. To pass a hug they say to whom and for what reason it is going, then gently squeeze the hand of the student next to them. The "squeeze" moves around the circle until it reaches its destination, at which point the receiver must acknowledge it, perhaps with a thank you.

You can start with something like, "I want to pass a hug to Sandy for finishing all her math today without having to be reminded to keep working." Once Sandy has received her "hug," it becomes her turn to send a hug to someone else. Initially, I thought this activity would work only with younger children, but have discovered that adolescents love the game too! Not only does it build positive self-concepts, but students also learn the importance of showing good manners and making positive statements to one another.

- Teach students how to give and accept constructive criticism. Practise this together in role-playing situations, using scenarios chosen by you. For example, "You know that Billy is planning to steal a chocolate bar from the store. What could you say?" Remember that the best way to teach the giving and accepting of constructive criticism is to model the behavior. So, when a student confronts you with a critical remark, turn it into a constructive criticism, accept it, and react appropriately. For example:

STUDENT: You never get our tests marked when you say you will.

TEACHER: Thank you for pointing out that I need to be better organized when I make promises to you. I can't promise to get them marked any faster, but I won't tell you to expect them before I'm *sure* I'll have them done.

You can also ask students for their advice on remedying any situation they criticize. For example, in the above scenario, you might ask if anyone has any suggestions about how you could get a few moments during class time to do some marking. Students will often make valid suggestions.

• Introduce a You Be the Teacher time, where students, on a rotating basis, take turns teaching a class of their choice. Allow them to choose any area of interest they have and are willing to share, as long as you approve the topic. Once, an introvert, ignored by all the other Grade 6 students, gave my class a wonderful lecture on stamp collecting. He shone for a full hour and was never quite so much a loner after that! Having students teach is especially great at Junior High, as long as those who don't want to are not forced to do so.

• Have students write specific weekly goals for themselves, write the goals in their journals or in specific Goal Books, then evaluate how well they have met their goals at the end of the week. You will have to teach the following:

1. How to write a specific goal that can be evaluated. For example: "I will get at least 80% on Friday's math test."
2. How to evaluate the goal. Did the student reach it completely? about half? not at all?
3. How to deal with a goal not yet reached. For example: "I will study 10 min more every night."

As for younger children, the teacher, aide, older "buddy," or parent will have to develop and write the goals for them, as well as help them to evaluate the goals, but beginning this training is never too early. The development of a positive self-concept relates directly to success and achievement such as is measured in the evaluation of how well a goal has been met. Once students learn to set, evaluate and learn from specific short-term goals, they can move toward more distant goals, such as passing the term, as well. The goals do not even need to be school-related, especially at first. One student, with a history of many failures, wrote, "I will brush my teeth 5 out of 7 nights this week." He even allowed for a couple of lapses on this simple goal and was ecstatic when he was able to rate his success at 100%. Little successes lead to bigger successes!

- Teach students to create a plan for reaching the goals they have set. You may have to do this in one-to-one situations initially (especially with younger children) but eventually, with practice, students will be able to write a goal on paper, list the necessary steps for its completion, implement the steps, and evaluate their progress. They may find it helpful to use a form such as the one below. The goal-setting procedure can be introduced in any subject area, although the simpler the goal the better during the learning stages. Here's an example.

GOAL SETTING

Name _____

Identify your goal: *I will get 80% on Friday's test.*

What steps will you take to reach your goal?

1. *Study 1 hr/night for 3 nights.*
2. *Do all homework.*
3. *Ask at least one question per class.*
4. *Find out exactly what I need to review for the test.*

Evaluate your goal: How close did you come to reaching it?

I got 78%. I almost reached my goal.

What part (if any) did you not achieve?

_____

What will you do about this in the next week/month?

I will study 10 min more each night.

When children can see themselves making and reaching goals, their self-concepts rise dramatically.

- Teach students how to put positive thoughts in their heads, perhaps referring to Norman Vincent Peale's book, *The Power of Positive Thinking*, for ideas on how to do this. If students can be taught to think positively, they are more likely to behave positively. For example, before a test when many students are thinking, "Oh, I just know I'm going to fail this test," teach them instead to say, "I know I'm going to pass this test." Point out that choice of thought is ours, and our strange and mysterious subconscious minds will react according to that thought, be it negative or positive. Always emphasize the power of positive thinking.

- Teach children to change their established self-images if they are unhappy with them by making specific affirmations for themselves. An affirmation is a one-sentence definition of a desired quality or trait. With your guidance, the students can follow these steps.

  1. Make an affirmation in the form of an "I" statement. Be both positive and specific. For example: "I am energetic."

  2. Read the words over, repeating them several times daily, and picture yourself having accomplished that goal.

  3. Imagine the feelings you will have when you achieve the goal. Try to read, picture and feel altogether.

  The form on page 29 can be used.

- After Junior High students have done the above exercise, explain to them that affirmations fall into categories of self-acceptance, growth, relationships, personality, health and skills. Let them try to categorize their own affirmations and possibly make one for each category. Doing this helps show students that they really do have the control and power to change themselves and create healthier self-concepts.

- Teach students to be assertive rather than aggressive. You may find *Discipline: Kids Are Worth It*, a tape by Barbara Coloroso, helpful. Role-play common scenarios, and demonstrate some assertive comebacks for them. By doing this you are giving students power over their own lives and consequently helping them to like themselves better.

- Teach relaxation techniques, such as muscle tension/relaxation (I recommend Janet Wessell's *Movement Fundamentals*); simple meditation techniques, such as imagining oneself in a peaceful place; and relaxation to music or taped voices.

AFFIRMATIONS...BEING A BETTER YOU!

WRITE YOUR "I" STATEMENT

I can/will/am _____

List the things you visualize happening when this is true.

1. _____

2. _____

3. _____

4. _____

List some of the feelings you will have when this is true.

1. _____

2. _____

3. _____

4. _____

Check each day that you concentrate on this affirmation.

Mon. _____ Tues. _____ Wed. _____ Thurs. _____ Fri. _____

Weekend Review: Write down any thoughts you have about your affirmation on the weekend.

_____

Optional: Circle the type of affirmation you believe this to be.
Remember that it may be more than one type.

Self-acceptance   Relationships
Personality   Specific skill(s)
Health   Other
Intellectual growth

- Have students make a chart of all their strengths in various areas such as school, sports, socialization, and crafts. At first, most will be hesitant to say they have *any* strengths for fear of being criticized by others, so help them get started by listing some of your own. Assure them that their lists will be confidential. You may find it necessary to help them by identifying a strength in each yourself or soliciting from the other students their assessments of each other's strengths. The idea behind this is to help students realize that they have strengths unique to them. In addition, when someone is having a particularly bad day, ask that student to reread his or her strengths list for the little lift it might provide. (I photocopy the lists for such occasions because students might not keep the originals.)

- Ask for, listen to, and respect the opinions of the students in areas of mutual concern (i.e., class rules). Students gain a sense of worth when they realize that their opinions matter and will be accepted even if they differ from those of teacher or peers. Teach respect for different views and opinions.
- Positive self-concept is directly related to group dynamics, the degree of acceptance within a group, plus the general cohesiveness and importance of the group. There are many ways in which to enhance the cohesiveness of your class as a group, which will, in turn, foster positive self-concepts among its members. Consider the following:

  a. Compete against another class (or school) in some athletic event where no special skills are required, eg., beachball volleyball.
  b. Fund-raise for a class function such as a class party or outing.
  c. Go to camp as a class.
  d. Make large advertisements, flags (use fabric crayons), or posters that draw attention to the merits of your class. Give your class a name, such as "Paterson's Pirates", or "Chow's Dragons," and have the students illustrate the name.
  e. Paint a large mural together. You can assign small sections to pairs of kids, then put all the sections together at the end. Oil pastels are an excellent medium for this assignment because of their rich vibrant colors.
  f. Create a tabletop environment of some sort with 3-D objects. We once created a wonderful science fiction mini-world in which burlap was moulded over mounds of sand to create an alien, moon-like surface; each student then added a 3-D structure, such as a foil-covered tower or dinky car or dome-shaped house of plasticine.
  g. Sit in a circle and tell a group story, where one person starts the story, then the next person picks it up, and so on.
  h. Go on a hike or a picnic just for the fun of it.
  i. Offer your class (Div. 2 or Jr. High) as buddies to a younger

class. Take them to the zoo, help them with homework, etc. For many years I had my Grade 6 class "pen pal" with a Grade 1 class in a different school. At the end of the year we all went to the zoo, with the "big kids" being totally responsible for the "little kids." Wonderful experience for all!

j. Write a class newspaper or build a class yearbook by saving good examples of students' writing, sketching, etc., throughout the year, then photocopying and coiling a copy for each student. You can include fun pages such as "Can you imagine..." or, "In the year 2001 we will...."

- When doing Language Arts assignments such as writing poetry, descriptions, and character analyses, have each student draw the name of another student and write about him/her, using only positives. These descriptions can later be shared with the whole class (after teacher screening, of course).
- Build self-concepts by giving students as much responsibility as possible. Allow them to make choices, and accept responsibility for the consequences of those choices without being "rescued" by you or their parents. You may find this difficult to do, but we all grow from our mistakes, so allowing students to make the wrong choices is really giving them respect, plus power over their own lives.
- Openly discuss emotions and the appropriate/inappropriate expression of these, so that kids learn they are not alone with their feelings. Doing so is important, because children, especially adolescents, often hide strong emotions; they fear rejection or other negative repercussions. They must be helped to realize that emotions are healthy and natural and that there are ways to deal with them appropriately. Have them role-play common scenarios (e.g., being rejected by peers or fighting with parents) and act out several possible coping strategies, discussing the feelings associated with each. In this way, the children will have some strategies the next time they are confronted with these situations, and will, therefore, feel more confident.

If you are to foster the growth of healthy self-concepts among your students, one final point must be remembered. Self-concepts are tied directly to the way persons who are important to us react. They are fragile, easily damaged, and difficult to repair. You, as the teacher, are a *very* significant other to each and every student, so don't take your role lightly. A callous word uttered in anger and without thought may be enough to shatter an already shaky self-concept. On the other hand, a smile and a word of acceptance and praise can have just the opposite effect. If you do slip up and say something you immediately wish you could take back (and don't we all?), then *take it back*. It's OK to say, "I was wrong. That was cruel of me. I apologize." Doing so can't undo the wrong, but can make it easier to bear. You have a lot of responsibility for the nurturing of your students' self-concepts, so, even though it may weigh heavily on you at times, be sure to look for shoots of promise and to believe always that everyone has potential.

B. Showing Respect

> **RESPECT:** to feel and show regard, esteem, consideration and appreciation.
>
> *Webster's II New Riverside Dictionary*

Showing respect to fellow human beings, regardless of age, sex, religion, race or socioeconomic standing, is a simple act of humanity. No doubt, every good teacher tries to instill it in his or her students. "Always treat your elders with respect." "Respect yourself and others will respect you." These pat phrases are easy to throw around, but like seeds tossed carelessly in the desert, most of them fall on barren ground.

Children learn by example! We know that. They build their repertoire of social skills from interactions with the significant adults in their lives. And few adults are more "significant" than teachers. If all this is true, then the question arises, "Why do students today tend to be disrespectful, not only to adults, but even to their peers?" Obviously there are many causes for this situation, with the breakdown of the traditional family being just one. Teachers, although they cannot alter these outside forces, can hope to have some good personal effects on students. In order to accomplish this, we must respect the students, not just when they are behaving appropriately and excelling academically, but *all* the time. An ancient Latin proverb avows, "The greatest respect is due children!" How painfully true.

"But of course I respect my students" is the foremost thought in the mind of every concerned teacher. And I believe we try.

But being fallible human beings we forget, and we make mistakes.

The following are examples of some teacher mistakes that we should watch out for and try to correct or avoid making.

- Scowling at a student is a blatant sign of disrespect. Although it may seem minor to the teacher, that simple, nonverbal act may harm the student who is already struggling with a less than adequate self-concept. So, if you find yourself starting to scowl, turn away, or try to change it to a smile.
- A word or two meant to stimulate or "shake up" a student can have the same untoward effect as a scowl. Consider these familiar putdowns:

  a. "How can you be so stupid?"
  b. "You weren't listening...again!"
  c. "You'll never amount to anything."
  d. "I don't know why I waste my time with you."

Would we be so free, I wonder, to fling such statements at our superiors or our peers? Probably not! Yet somehow we sometimes believe that our students deserve them, and, indeed, can handle them without filing them away as examples of open disrespect. We do not set out to show disrespect to our students, but too often that's exactly what happens. And the students, in turn, model our behavior. So, be prepared to bite your tongue. Or, if hurtful words have already escaped, apologize and change them. You can't undo what has been done, but you can lessen the impact somewhat. Think before speaking.

However, we engage in an extremely stressful occupation which often doesn't allow us the luxury of reflection. We teachers can be easily hurt, angered and frustrated by those very students we are supposed to respect. Nonetheless, we presumably have more control over the classroom than our students do. There are three steps we can take to help us remember to respect our students.

1. Be more aware of what you are saying and doing in the classroom. Everything the teacher says and does has an impact on the students. The evidence of this may not be readily observable, but it is true nonetheless.

2. Take the time, just a few moments a day, to praise each student verbally. At the Junior High level where the teacher sees

perhaps hundreds of students each day, recognize the worth of different students daily.

3. Always keep in mind that these young people with whom we are in contact every day are just that — people. They are real, feeling, human beings, who will one day be ruling the world and taking care of us! Let us respect them for they are, truly, our tomorrows!

C. Teaching Independence

A school should not be preparation for life.
A school should be life!

— *Elbert Hubbard*

Teaching excellence lies in the ability of the teacher to help the students manage without him or her — to learn on their own — to become self-motivated and, eventually, self-sufficient. Doing so is difficult because the entire teacher/student relationship, if it is effective, tends to foster dependence. Therefore, we must try, consciously, to reduce this dependence and promote independence and responsibility. There are several ways a teacher can do so. They are not directly a part of any given curriculum, but, given the flexibility within most curricula, can be justified under almost any skill or content area.

The teaching of techniques such as are listed here is based on the belief that, although the curriculum may not demand it, teachers are responsible for guiding the "whole child." For five hours a day, your students are a captive audience; use your time with them wisely, so that they are ready for life with more than just math skills or word definitions. It is your moral obligation, as a teacher, to teach *life*!

- **DAILY LIFE SKILLS:** At Junior High we incorporate many of these in Home Economics and Industrial Arts, but why not begin at the elementary level? Young children can be taught to sew on a button, sew up seams, iron, follow a recipe, etc. Many students do not get these experiences at home, and even those who do thoroughly enjoy reviewing them with peers.
- **BABYSITTING:** Grade 5 and 6 students appreciate a course, right in their classroom, on babysitting. Sometimes, you can arrange for outside instructors to come in. Students may pass

a test and receive an official babysitting certificate (check with the YMCA). If such a course is unavailable, the school nurse or the community health nurse will surely help you to set up and implement one. An excellent (and thoroughly amusing — don't forget your camera) conclusion to this "course" is to arrange for babies of various ages to be brought into your class to spend the afternoon. Their parents can demonstrate the techniques of diaper changing, bottle feeding and so forth, and your students will gain a wonderful real-life learning experience. (Just watch how some boys handle the babies — it's hilarious!)

- **TALKING TO ADULTS:** Many children seldom talk to adults other than their teachers and parents. Talking to adults is not a skill that comes naturally or easily to many of them, so consider helping them to develop and refine the skill. Role-playing scenarios, such as asking/giving directions, talking to parents' friends, or sitting beside a strange adult during a long trip, can be very helpful to otherwise shy or overbearing children. Children can be coached to listen carefully and without interruption, use eye contact, be polite and respectful, ask questions, avoid gossiping, whining or complaining, and show interest in what an adult is saying. They can then improve their communication skills greatly. An excellent conclusion to this activity is to either invite elderly adults to the classroom for discussions, or take your class to a senior citizens' home. Both young and old will be delighted with the results.

- **COMMUNICATION SKILLS:** Many books and references deal with communication skills, so I will just briefly delineate a few major points (in addition to those mentioned in the preceding paragraph), of which children of all grade levels should be made aware: body language; concentration; expression of honest feelings; honesty; asking for clarification or help; paraphrasing; listening attentively; saying what you mean — meaning what you say!

    Many games can be applied to this area, for example, charades (body language and nonverbal communication), whisper (sometimes called telephone line or gossip), and improvisations of life situations.

- **CHILDREN AND THE LAW:** Help ensure that students of all grade levels hear lessons on such issues as kidnapping, shoplifting, vandalism, and sexual harassment. You can also play a role in acquainting Junior High students with the Young

Offenders Act and its implications. If you are uncomfortable with or unknowledgeable about any of these topics, seek outside help. There are many avenues open to you. The police are willing and eager to give presentations; the John Howard Society will present a complete package on children and the law. Arrange for these experts to come and give your students the information they need.

- **GROOMING:** Within the context of the Health curriculum, teachers usually teach cleanliness and dental care to their students. What I am recommending here is to extend this teaching to include such areas as poise, walking or sitting properly, dressing appropriately for different occasions as well as for different body types, and using deodorant and shampoo regularly. For example, you may be able to help a Junior High student with body odor by suggesting the use of a good deodorant. Teaching of this nature may seem frivolous to many educators, but I have found that students from about Grade 4 on not only enjoy and appreciate it, but learn much about themselves and the image they present to others. Bringing in a professional, such as a "model," adds flair. After a part-time model visited a Grade 6 class to speak on deportment, most of the typical slouches of 10-year-olds disappeared and were replaced by wonderful straight backs.

- **ETIQUETTE:** Although many students are taught the rules of etiquette at home, many more are not. If we remember that education has, for its objective, the formation of character, the teaching of etiquette is readily justifiable. Many books and resources are available to assist in this area. Role-playing situations in which students are likely to find themselves seems to be a good way to approach the subject. Remember to tell students *why* they need to understand and use our society's rules of etiquette. At the Junior High level, you might want to compare our rules with those of some other societies. For example, belching loudly is not only very appropriate in some places, but is actually expected.

- **SMOKING, DRUGS AND ALCOHOL:** Although a primary grade teacher should be prepared to deal with questions on these matters, discussion related to them is generally limited to Division 2 and Junior High. Here, again, call on outside help such as the school nurse, a doctor, or even an Alcoholics Anonymous representative. Grade 5 is not too soon to acquaint students with the dangers of substance abuse. In fact, many children by this time have already had first-hand experience. One useful technique is to role-play situations where students are exposed to peers who are encouraging them to "try it!" The students can then experiment with ways in which to decline the offer without incurring mockery, teasing or even threats. For example, through role playing or simply discussing the issue, students will probably come up with such responses as "I've tried it and don't like it" and "I'm allergic to it!"

- **JOB RESPONSIBILITIES:** Elementary teachers don't usually concern themselves with this area of life preparation; they feel their students are too young. Consider, however, that many children have part-time jobs such as babysitting, cutting lawns, and shovelling snow. Discussing such matters as being on time, being efficient and dependable, and being polite can be relevant. Skills learned at this age will assist students later in life when keeping a job will be essential. A good way to approach this topic is to make, with the students' assistance, a chart delineating job responsibilities. In addition to how to behave at work, students through role playing learn how to present themselves when applying for a job. At the Junior High level, you can provide pointers on how to complete a job application form and write a résumé.

- **WELLNESS THROUGH KEEPING FIT:** Although this comes primarily under the physical education curriculum, its importance merits mentioning in all other areas as well. The 1990s have brought a new awareness of the values of physical fitness and many new and interesting ways to achieve fitness. Yet especially at Junior High level, it seems students are prone to lying around in front of a TV set for hours at a time. Let's bring a positive outlook on physical well-being into the classroom and stress the importance of regular exercise. Many fitness experts would be glad to talk to students of any age and offer suggestions on what they can do to keep fit. And you can incorporate fitness activities into your regular curriculum. Instead of taking a bus to the zoo, walk there. Or if it's too far, walk part way and have the bus pick you up. Begin a daily exercise-to-music break in your morning and assign different students to lead each day. Have students keep journals of their weekly exercise activities. Doing this creates an awareness of just how little some of them are doing, and being aware is the first step. Of course, the teacher must set a good example. Don't drag yourself up those stairs — jog! And smile, it's for your own good!

- **SHOWING APPRECIATION:** All children know how to say thank you, but few know how to go beyond this to show their appreciation for both things and for more abstract gifts such as time, comfort or support. Teach them to write short thank-you notes, to make thank-you calls, to send little cards or small tokens of appreciation, to show, in any way they can think of, their appreciation. Once students get into the habit of doing this, the results they witness will be reinforcement to continue the behavior. A good place to begin is right in the school where the students can write little notes of appreciation to custodians, lunch supervisors, aides, secretaries, the principal, etc. Encourage the students to be specific in their thanks, and watch the smiles of appreciation on the faces of the receivers.

- **MONEY MANAGEMENT:** Teach children how to handle their money — even many high school students don't know how to use a bank. A visit from a banker can be very effective. Let children write (phony) cheques, fill in deposit slips, and balance budgets at as young an age as possible. If the class participates in a fund-raising project, then they can gain valuable money-managing experience.

- **FIRST AID AND EMERGENCIES:** All students, regardless of age, would benefit from learning a minimum of emergency first-aid techniques. Again, the school or community nurse can be very helpful, as can the Red Cross or St. John Ambulance societies; they will often provide free demonstrations geared to the ages of your students. Along with this, teach students how to behave in emergency situations such as being locked out of the house, getting lost, being sexually harassed, being home alone unexpectedly, and providing emergency first aid to oneself.

- **CHARTS:** As a final task in life preparation, have each student make a small, neat phone number chart that they can take home and mount near the phone. The chart should include the usual emergency phone numbers in addition to the names and numbers of several significant adults whom they could call if necessary. Some students even like to make smaller, wallet-sized cards to carry with them. The goal is to show students that they are not alone, and that help is always available from some source. This recognition gives them a sense of power and independence which is necessary for survival in today's world.

'Tis education forms the common mind;
Just as the twig is bent, the tree's inclined.
— *Alexander Pope*

D. Determining Logical (and Palatable) Consequences

Everyone stood in awe of the lion tamer in the cage, with half a dozen lions all under the control of his "consequences." Everyone, that is, except the teacher...

— *June Dostal*

Today we hear so much about logical consequences, that the expression has almost become a cliché. Every teacher knows the importance of logical consequences and the rationale for their use. Every teacher has had first-hand experience with logical consequences, for example, the copy machine breaks when you have left the test you need for the next period until the last minute to copy. However, the concern of this section is not serious logical consequences for the teacher, but the establishment of serious logical consequences for the student. This, as every teacher will know only too well, is not always easy. The problem arises when, during that split second of time when a viable consequence must be offered by the teacher, the mind draws a blank. A little voice reminds you that you can't say, "... or you'll stay here all night to finish it," (who's going to stay all night with the culprit?); "Stop that or I'll never speak to you again" (really?); or "Next time, I'll hit you back," (teachers aren't allowed to hit, remember?). So, what are some logical and palatable consequences that are workable for you and that won't embarrass the student? The following suggestions may be useful. However, remember that every situation is as unique as the children involved; what works for one may not work for another. Trial and error is the only technique I know to establish the effectiveness of any consequence. What, for instance, would be the logical consequence here?

STUDENT: (to Teacher) Do you think it's right to punish people for things they didn't do?

TEACHER: Of course not.

STUDENT: Good, because I didn't do my homework!

Sometimes the most logical consequence is laughter! Sometimes, our students really do outsmart us, and admitting and accepting that is great. Still, having in one's repertoire a few possible consequences upon which to draw is useful. The following have been tried with varying degrees of success. Use them with caution, with "either/or" choices, for example, "Either you get your homework done on time or... (consequence)."

Remember that your role is to ensure that the consequence, should the student choose it, is carried out. The choice is always the student's, but the consistency is the teacher's! If the student refuses to make a choice when presented with an either/or statement, then give him or her the benefit of the doubt and verbally choose the most appropriate choice, using an expression such as "I assume from your silence that you have chosen ____."

Since effective consequences are dependent upon the age (and, of course, interests) of the students involved, I have tried to indicate the division levels of the following consequences (Div. 1 = Grades 1, 2, 3; Div. 2 = Grades 4, 5, 6; JH = Grades 7, 8, 9). In addition, because students always need to know *why* a specific consequence has been given, the rationales are provided.

PROBLEM BEHAVIOR: Fighting at recess, noons...

- Send the fighters to separate places on the playground for the next two or more recesses and forbid them from interacting with their peers in any way. RATIONALE: To learn how others get along without fighting. (Div. 1 or 2)
- Have them miss the next two recesses, by remaining in some nonreinforcing area without your attention. RATIONALE: Time out to think about getting along and solving problems in a more acceptable manner. (Div. 1 or 2)
- Ask the students to write reports at subsequent recesses or noons about "Fighting in History" (eg., Vietnam War). RATIONALE: To realize the futility of fighting to solve problems. (Div. 2 and JH)

    NOTE: English teachers may object to report writing as a consequence for negative behavior, but if the emphasis is on the content rather than the English, such writing appears to be a useful tool — often quite enlightening to the student!

PROBLEM BEHAVIOR: Fighting in classroom or hall

- Have the fighters sit on the floor, facing each other but about 2 m apart (out of "striking" distance but well within eye contact); neither student may get up and return to class, go to the bathroom, get a drink...whatever...until the other one gives permission to do so. All time missed while they glare at each other and try to reach a mutual agreement must be made up *after* class. (Discipline expert Barbara Coloroso advocates this technique.) RATIONALE: Co-operation is necessary if students are to solve their own problems. They may never come to an agreement about anything other than allowing each other to get up, but that's a start! (Div. 1, 2 and JH)
- Give a pencil to one student and paper to the other, and ask for a written account of what happened. (As before, missed class time must be made up later.) RATIONALE: Co-operation, listening skills, and thought processes are heightened. (Div. 2 and JH)
- Isolate the students from all reinforcement and activity. Find a secluded time or place. Some teachers place a desk in the corner or hall and block it off with cardboard. Others have used the nurse's room (if it is empty). I even knew one effective teacher who found a storage room filled with "junk," cleaned it out, put a gym mat on the floor, and used it efficiently as a "time-out room." Just be sure to state how long the student must remain there — *don't* lock the student in, and don't forget to go back and get him or her! RATIONALE: Time to think about one's behavior and/or to get under control. (Div. 1, 2 and JH)
- Physically restrain the child. Hold the student in a tight, yet gentle position, perhaps with arms crossed and held from behind, and talk calmly to him or her until calm prevails. Sometimes the mere physical closeness of the teacher is enough to get a vicious temper tantrum under control, plus restraining the child prevents injury to other students. RATIONALE: "I will control you until you can control yourself. I care about you." (Div. 1)

PROBLEM BEHAVIOR: Swearing or name calling

These antisocial behaviors have no logical consequences that avoid embarrassment to the acting-up student. There are simply consequences that look suspiciously like punishments. For example, consider the age-old washing-the-mouth-out-with-soap response to swearing. At first glance this treatment may appear to be logical, but upon closer examination it can be recognized as a punishment. You can respond to antisocial behaviors, however, but following the rules of logical and natural consequences may not be possible.

- Call for a time-out in a predesignated place. RATIONALE: To think about what was said and to prepare to explain why it was/is unacceptable. (Div. 1, 2, and JH)
- Have the student research and write a report on why swearing is objectionable to others, the work to be done daily, before or after school, until completed to the teacher's satisfaction. RATIONALE: Student is forced to realize why swearing is unacceptable. (Div. 2 and JH).
- Request the student to write a list of all the possible alternatives to swearing, for example, use of a nonsense word or biting the tongue. RATIONALE: Student may choose to do something other than swear the next time an annoying situation occurs. (Div. 2 and JH)

  NOTE: Forcing an apology from a student who has engaged in swearing or name calling accomplishes nothing. The student becomes angry, and you would mistakenly feel you've done all you could.

PROBLEM BEHAVIOR: Talking out in class

- Ignore the student and call on a nearby student to answer. RATIONALE: Student gets the message vicariously and realizes that he/she needs to raise a hand in order to be acknowledged. (Div. 1 and 2; this *may* work at JH, but as a rule it seems to intensify the talker's level of speech.)
- Move quietly to the student after giving the entire class an assignment, and privately discuss the behavior, giving a consequence if it occurs again. RATIONALE: Student is neither embarrassed nor reinforced in front of peers, but is told what to expect should the incident reoccur. (Div. 1, 2 and JH)
- After a warning, remove the loud student from class with a

minimum of arguing, pleading, pulling, etc., which is reinforcing. Use a predesignated place, perhaps a secluded desk
in a colleague's classroom. There, you can avoid peer reinforcement, but have another teacher watching. Time missed from
your class is, naturally, made up later. RATIONALE: Student's
behavior is having a detrimental effect on the class as well as
his or her own performance. A time-out will give the student
an opportunity to develop self-control and get ready to work.
(Div. 2 and JH)

PROBLEM BEHAVIOR: Homework not done

- Make the student remain inside at recess times to complete
  homework. RATIONALE: Student has chosen to work at school
  rather than at home, so you provide the time and the place.
  (Div. 2 and JH)
- Cut a prespecified number of marks off the final grade.
  RATIONALE: Student has chosen to lose the marks rather than
  do the homework. You are putting the responsibility for the
  work on the student...where it belongs! (JH)
- Tell the student to leave class immediately and complete homework (hall, library, peer's room...), then be responsible for
  obtaining work missed and putting in an equal amount of time
  after school. RATIONALE: Homework is given priority over
  other work at this time. (Div. 2 and JH)
- Use a Homework Book, a daily record of work to be done,
  signed by both teachers and parents. The student is responsible for filling it in; the teacher merely initials the records, as
  do the parents. RATIONALE: Total home/school communication.
  The assumption is that the student can't, at this time, be totally
  responsible for homework completion. External motivation to
  do homework is necessary; parents are aware of the school's
  expectations and can react as they see fit. (Div. 2 and JH)

PROBLEM BEHAVIOR: Throwing (snowball, paper planes, gum or
paper wads...whatever)

- Have the thrower spend at least one recess/noon watching
  others without participating at all. RATIONALE: Learning other
  ways to play (Div. 1, 2 and JH)
- Isolate the student for a specific amount of time (recess/noons)
  to think and document all the reasons why throwing is not
  allowed, then have the thrower share these reasons with an

adult, at a predetermined time. RATIONALE: Student may come to understand the dangers of throwing and perhaps stop the behavior. (Div. 2 and JH)

PROBLEM BEHAVIOR: Playing with something irrelevant during class, for example, listening to a walkman or putting on make-up

- Ask that the item be put on your desk for safekeeping. Since doing so may cause an argument with a Junior High student, give the student a choice, "Put it away, or put it on my desk." (Usually the student will choose to put it away, but if not, you are into a power struggle, not dealt with here.) RATIONALE: Teacher will keep item until a more appropriate time. (Div. 1, 2 and JH, with JH modifications)
- After a warning, confiscate the item for a specific time. The best way to do this is to move as inconspicuously as possible to the guilty party and quietly take the item, explaining why you are taking it, and when it will be returned.
  NOTE: It then becomes your responsibility not to lose the item. For instance, leaving someone's treasure on your desk is inviting trouble. You may have to explain to the student, and possibly even to the parents, how you managed to lose the object. RATIONALE: Student needs time without the distraction of the item. (Div. 1, 2 and JH)
- Share the item with the class, especially if it is something like candy or a joke book. RATIONALE: If the item is important enough to require the student's attention, then it's important enough for the entire group's attention.
  NOTE: Be aware that this particular consequence could be misused by a student who simply *wants* to disrupt the class. Know your students!

PROBLEM BEHAVIOR: Talking back to the teacher (rude or disrespectful behavior)

- Calmly explain why you will not accept that behavior, and ask the student to go to the predesignated time-out area. Tell the student to return when he or she can show self-control. If the child does not return within a fairly brief time, go to the area and discuss the behavior. RATIONALE: You need to establish control, and the student needs time to review his or her behavior. (Div. 2 and JH)
- Ignore the behavior and give obvious reinforcement to another

student who is exhibiting the opposite behavior, eg., "Jody, I appreciate your polite manner of talking. It demonstrates your maturity." RATIONALE: You are not reinforcing the inappropriate behavior by acknowledging it, but the student will still get the message. (Div. 1, 2 and JH)

- Send the student to the counsellor to discuss respect and the appropriate way to speak to others. (Some children don't even realize when they are being rude!) Missed class time will be made up. RATIONALE: Student needs assistance in understanding why his or her behavior is not acceptable and in finding different means of communicating. (Div. 2 and JH)

PROBLEM BEHAVIOR: Stealing little items such as pens or larger ones such as money and clothes. A major concern when it comes to stealing is knowing for certain the identity of the culprit. If in doubt, never make an accusation! Doing so can only lead to irreparable damage for both student and teacher. But sometimes the student will admit involvement or is caught red-handed.

- Request that the student return or replace items. RATIONALE: Student accepts responsibility and makes restitution. (Div. 1, 2 and JH)
- Instruct the student to research and write a report, to be presented to peers, on the Young Offenders Act. RATIONALE: Although a curriculum area is involved in the consequence, the merits validate the procedure. The student(s) learn first-hand, valuable information that is directly pertinent to them. (Div. 2 and JH)
- Arrange for a visit from the local police force (they are always willing as they have special branches for just this sort of thing) to talk about stealing and its consequences. Have the student accused of or suspected of theft responsible for meeting, greeting and introducing the police. RATIONALE: Again, first-hand information for the student(s), plus additional responsibility for the specific student. (Div. 1, 2 and JH)
- Ensure the student visits a local courtroom and witnesses and reports on a theft charge. RATIONALE: Same as above. (Div. 1, 2 and JH)
- Sometimes, especially with younger children, constant theft of small objects such as crayons may mean that the student doesn't have those items and has no other way of obtaining them. Check the situation carefully, then talk with the student

one on one. You can make some sort of deal whereby, in exchange for the necessary items, the student helps you with such chores as keeping the boards clean. Just remember to show the student respect by making these arrangements in private and check your board's policy on such use of supplies. Expect to spend some of your own money when making the arrangements. RATIONALE: The student earns the desired items. (Div. 1)

PROBLEM BEHAVIOR: Late for school (a lot)

Many schools have a specific late policy which, of course, must be followed, but you can provide additional consequences as well.

- Do something of interest or importance immediately after the bell. For example, tell a joke, or answer a riddle given the previous day. The late student could also miss information on an upcoming assignment or test or even an actual question from the test; tell the students present they cannot share the information with latecomers. One example that works well with older students is to tell them to do only the even numbers on a page, then not mention that to latecomers who end up doing all the page's questions. With younger children, simply handing out a little treat to eat right after the bell is enough. RATIONALE: Students will soon want to be on time so as not to miss something. (Div. 1, 2 and JH)
- Make late students remain outside the classroom until either the end of the period, or until you choose to find a natural break. Missed time must be made up after school. RATIONALE: Students learn that interrupting is bad manners. (Div. 2 and JH)
- Arrange with parents for the student to go to bed earlier, the number of minutes to be determined by the number of minutes he/she tends to be late, eg., John is usually 10 min late for class, so he must be in bed 10 min earlier. RATIONALE: Student must be too tired to get to school on time. (Div. 1, 2)

PROBLEM BEHAVIOR: Being out of seat

Before reading this section, please remember that young children are very active, and long periods of seat work may be unrealistic. (Of course, I can say the same thing of adolescents!) However, when children must remain in their seats, at least for a while, there are some solutions.

- Move Mr. Activity's desk to an isolated area (hall, carrel) for a specific length of time. RATIONALE: Student will be less of a distraction to others and possibly be less distracted by them. (Div. 1)
- Keep a record of out-of-seat time, and have the child make up all that time after school. RATIONALE: Being out of seat is equivalent to time off the job and must, therefore, be made up. (Div. 2 and JH)

  NOTE: Since this intervention requires monitoring by someone to keep track of the out-of-seat time, it becomes less palatable. Soliciting the help of a parent, aide or peer may make it easier.
- Introduce the use of row monitors (usually the worst offenders are the best monitors). Monitors strive to keep the others in their rows seated. A kind of "Row Challenge" will work once in a while. The activity is best when you really have to keep those students in their desks for a specified length of time, for example, for a test. You'll need some sort of reward for the winning row. RATIONALE: Peer pressure works!

PROBLEM BEHAVIOR: The class clown disrupts class with jokes, funny faces, falling out of desks, noises...

- Stop teaching with a statement such as, "I can see ____ is entertaining again. OK, you have a choice. You may come to the front and entertain us all for 3 min then stop, or you may stop now." (CAUTION: As with all interventions, you must know your students well. If several clowns choose to entertain the class, considerable teaching time could be lost; but if one child entertains for 3 min, little time has been lost and a potentially disastrous situation has been diffused.) RATIONALE: The clown gets the required attention and is allowed to make a choice, the class is returned to order, and you remain in control. (Div. 1, 2 and JH)
- Call for a time-out, with all the same conditions as previously mentioned time-outs. You might say, "You are disrupting the class and bothering me. Please leave until you are under control and able to work quietly. You may go to —." It is important to state specifically *where* the student is to go, even if it's just to the hall outside your door; otherwise, you are giving the student free rein of the school, which will only compound the existing problem. (CAUTION: Do not forget the student.

Most students, when given the choice of returning "when they are ready," will soon come back, but of course, one will try to disappear. You are still responsible for that student, so check on him or her often!) RATIONALE: To give the student an opportunity to get under control. (Div. 2 and JH)

Remember that for every inappropriate behavior you have to react to, you probably could, and should, have reacted to instances of appropriate behavior first. For example, if the class clown has been quietly behaving well for some time, praise him or her; do not wait for a lapse. Choose *action* rather than reaction, *prevention* rather than intervention! But if a consequence for inappropriate behavior is necessary, make it as logical as possible and palatable to you, and present it in the form of an either/or statement, so that the choice is left to the student. Then follow through, doing exactly what you said you would.

In the end, however, all we can hope to do is to make it easier for the child to choose our way of behaving rather than another way less acceptable to us. The final decision belongs to the child!

CHAPTER 3

Communicating

A. Communicating Verbally

It's not what we say, but how we say it that packs the punch!

Every teacher knows that communicating verbally is a primary teaching tactic, but I wonder how many of us really understand its significance. Consider, for example, the difference between saying, "You look like a breath of spring." and "You look like the end of a hard, cold winter." Although the meanings are the same, the choice of words provides an entirely different connotation to each statement! Children, not as sophisticated as we are, take words at face value. Because of this, I have, largely as a result of making heinous errors myself, created a brief list of cautions for teachers.

- Never end a statement of acceptance, acknowledgment, or agreement with "but." As soon as that little three-letter word is uttered, the entire previous phrase is wiped out. Consider the following. "I am glad to see you are on time today...but...if you are late again I will have to contact your parents!" All the student hears and remembers is the latter part of the statement which was meant, originally, as positive reinforcement. Forget the "buts"! Bite your tongue as soon as you hear yourself starting to "but." If it's too late and That Word has already been uttered, quickly change the ending. You could say, "I am glad you are on time today...but...I'll be even happier when you are on time tomorrow!"
- Give verbal praise liberally. Praise is a device for making children deserve it, and it works! Of course, the praise *must* be specific and sincere. Rather than say, "Good work," try, "Good work, Jill. You have done all the division steps in order." Children need to know exactly what it is they have done correctly or incorrectly.

- Some people speak twice before they think! Teachers are human, and sometimes we say something that we immediately wish we could swallow. But all is not lost! You always have the chance to apologize, retract the remark by admitting you were wrong, or even just say something like, "I can't believe I said that silly thing!" The beauty of teaching is that you always get a second chance. Use it!
- Be careful to talk to students, no matter what age they are, with respect. Nothing is more distasteful to students than being talked down to. Students don't want to be treated like children (even though they *are*) and will quickly turn off and tune out any adult who talks to them as if they don't understand. Tone of voice is as important as word choice. Try to talk to students as you would your peers.
- Be aware of the incredibly complicated nature of our language, and realize that students may not have the experience to make meaning of ambiguous words correctly. Puns exemplify the problem. Someone might wonder, "Why can we catch a cold, but not a warm?" Check for understanding when talking to students. The more abstract the conversation, the more checks for understanding are needed.
- Be aware of the quality of your own voice. Although you probably cultivated an acceptable voice during training, you might want to check it periodically. Simply tape yourself for an entire day. Then listen to the recording critically. Does your voice have pleasant pitches and intonations? Do you talk too quickly? too slowly? Do you notice that toward the end of the day your voice becomes more whiny or "short"? If you notice any disagreeable qualities — change them! Being aware of the problem is the first step. And believe me, you can make drastic changes in your voice! I once worked with a student teacher whose voice was so squeaky and high-pitched that the students cringed when she spoke. The student teacher and I worked together on voice exercises, etc., and by the end of six weeks, she had not only lowered the decibel level of her voice, but had created a lovely, soft-spoken, even sexy way of communicating. So listen to yourself! Would *you* like to be a captive audience in your class all day? If the answer is "no," then make some changes!

Talking is what we, as teachers, do. Let's do it well!

B. Communicating Nonverbally

Teachers tend to be masters of the art of nonverbal communication — and they need to be. Students quickly become skillful interpreters of nonverbal cues. Every student knows the teacher's mood the minute the teacher walks in the room. Every student is aware of those particular times when rules can be stretched and jokes enjoyed. And every student knows when to be quiet, but may not necessarily *be* quiet!

You need to be sure your body language matches your words. If you say, "Feel free to come to me for help," but are standing with arms folded tightly to body, legs rigid, your invitation will not be convincing. Similarly, trying to regain control of an unruly class while slouching in your desk with your feet up and your hands behind your head will be unsuccessful. But we know these things, so a simple reminder is sufficient.

If you feel comfortable with the idea, you might ask your students to mime you. As long as you are open-minded, you can learn much. Students are masters at picking up those little idiosyncrasies we don't even realize we have and exploiting them. For instance, I never knew that I always leaned on the left side of my desk when waiting for them to get their readers out! However, bear in mind the personalities of your students and assess the benefits of the exercise against the risks to your own ego before you open yourself up.

Signals

Teachers require specific means by which to get the attention of the whole class quickly and easily. What they can rely on is signals, cues that focus attention. For a signal to be used effectively, the students must be trained to react in a specific way. Training requires explaining and modelling the signal and reinforcing the appropriate response. It usually takes a relatively short time to accomplish. Once a class is properly trained, use of the signal will trigger a genuine conditioned response.

Remember that signals are grade specific. What will work with Kindergarten and Division 1 students will probably seem silly to Division 2 students and ridiculous to "mature" Junior High students. Therefore, these cues have suggested divisions following them.

- **MUSIC:** Select a specific piece of instrumental music ("Pink

Panther'' or ''Baby Elephant Walk'' work well) and have it read-ily available on tape. When students hear the music, they immediately stop what they are doing, return to their desks, and put their heads down. You do not have to play the entire piece every time, although I found that younger children often want me to let the song continue till the end. (Div. 1)

- **SONG:** Begin singing a popular song, known by all. Students join in and begin putting away their work as they sing. By the end of the song, all should be seated, awaiting new directions. (Div. 1)

- **WHISPER:** Begin whispering *anything* to nearby students. Soon all will have stopped to listen (natural curiosity is a wonder here). You might whisper jokes, questions from the next quiz, silly instructions such as ''put your finger on your nose'' (with this one, it's easy to see who is listening), or directions. (Any grade...especially JH)

- **LIGHTS:** Most teachers use this technique of flicking the lights off and on. But there can be some refinement of the signal. Lights off and remaining off could mean that students return to their desks. Blinking lights could mean that they freeze where they are. (Div. 1 and 2)

- **ARM RAISE:** Stand in a central location and silently raise one arm. As students begin to spot you, they, too, freeze and raise an arm. Soon all are in this position, ready to listen. (Div 1 and 2)

- **CLAPS:** Two loud claps might mean ''stop and listen.'' Usually one clap is not enough because students may not hear it; too many claps become bothersome. You can, however, have different directions associated with different numbers of claps. (Div. 1)

- **COUNTDOWN:** Using visible hand signals as well as your voice, begin a loud countdown from 3. By the time you get to 1 the expectation is that all noise will have ceased. (JH)

- **WHISTLE CODE:** Especially effective for outdoor activities, such as hikes or Physical Education. However, a whistle can also be used with any noisy activity (e.g., art, drama, group work). One blow of the whistle might mean ''stop, freeze''; two blows, ''return to your places''; three blows, ''go immediately to the person with the whistle.'' (Div. 2 and JH)

- **INSTRUMENT CODE:** Use any handy rhythm-band or musical instrument the way you would a whistle. Suitable instruments are the xylophone, triangle, bells, rhythm sticks, and tambourine. The specific instrument can be changed at regular intervals for the sake of variety. "This month our freeze and listen signal will be the shake of the tambourine." The instruments can also be season- or theme-related, for example, jingle bells in December, the xylophone for spring raindrops, rhythm sticks for Halloween skeletons, and so forth. (Div. 1 and 2)

- **TEACHER TIME-OUT:** Sometimes, the class gets out of control and you just don't know what to do. Take a time-out. Leave the classroom, quietly and with poise, and remain outside for several minutes. The effect of this action is usually quite dramatic. Students are human too, and they really don't want to upset you to this extent. Use caution, though. This technique must not be overused! (Any grade, but most powerful at JH)

You will probably use a variety of other signals, as well. Many of these are gestures, such as putting a finger to the lips for "quiet," and putting up a hand for "stop." Note that even for these common signals, you should plan to train your students how to respond so that signal use will be most effective. Common signals, such as those outlined below, are often directed at an individual rather than an entire class.

- A wink, an obvious act of approval, works wonders.
- Tapping or cupping the ear with the hand means "speak louder please."
- Making a horizontal wave motion with the hand means "slow down." The signal is especially useful in public speaking, report giving, and drama.)
- Raised eyebrows mean "do you need help?"
- An exaggerated nod indicates approval or agreement.
- An open hand means "stop!" A closed fist means "go!"
- Clicking fingers mean "look at me."

It is not the innovativeness of the signal that makes it work (although that helps), but the consistency of its use after an adequate training period. Use of a signal must be followed by a pause to allow for the appropriate response; it must also be followed up by a word or two of appreciation matched with body language. A simple "thanks" will do. But even better would be a more specific comment, for example, "Thank you all for remembering to sit down when you heard the music. That makes me happy."

53

Remember, children have more need of models than of critics, so if they do not respond to your signal properly, model it again.

C. Marking Students' Work

> Too often students are given answers to remember,
> rather than problems to solve.
>
> — *Roger Lewin*

"To mark or not to mark" is something with which teachers often wrestle. Given the multitude of responsibilities and duties delegated to them (us), marking hundreds of pages of work often seems like an onerous task. It's rather like housework — neverending — and with about the same amount of intrinsic pleasure. However, if students are to appreciate the importance of learning, of completing assignments, and of generally being accountable for their work, marking is essential. Given this truism, each teacher must adopt a method of marking that works for him or her. The following suggestions may fit into your method; they have worked for me.

- **SPOT-CHECK**: If you simply can't mark all the work, either spot-check, that is, mark random questions, or sign or initial the work to indicate you have looked at it. You might want a signature stamp which is fast to use and looks important. You will thereby make students realize you will look at everything they do; they are made accountable. And you can avoid hearing, "We don't have to do ____, 'cause she never checks anyway."
- **MARK NEATLY**: Use small checks or x's, making sure the x's are not twice as big as the checks. (I have often caught myself creating ugly, huge x's on students' work.) Remember that even in marking, you are modelling neatness and affecting the self-esteem of your students.
- **MARK IT WRONG**: If an answer is wrong, mark it so! Marking "partly correct" or "almost right" only confuses the student, unless, of course, you provide clearly the missing or incorrect part of the answer. Even then, this type of marking falls dangerously into the "yes — BUT!" type of comment discussed earlier in this chapter.
- **MAKE SPECIFIC COMMENTS**: Always comment specifically on work well done. Instead of saying "good work," say, "You

know all your punctuation. Good! Now you will be able to make your writing more understandable." Tell students why their knowledge will be valuable to them.

- **REMARK:** If you mark something wrong, expect it to be corrected and remarked. Otherwise, marking is a waste of time. Something wrong indicates something in need of reteaching and redoing. Keep a Remark Record, a record of students' work that will require another look (see example). Let students know they must correct errors and show you again. Follow through. Doing so is difficult, but is very important. Keep students accountable — especially those in Junior High!

REMARK RECORD

Name	Assignment	First Date	First Mark	Comments	Redo Date	Mark
Sue	Fantasy story 500 words	Jan.5	35%	200 words no conclusion spelling untidy	Jan.15 ✓	60%
Carol	Fantasy story 500 words	Jan.5	50%	poor grammar punctuation	Jan.15 X	not handed back in yet

- **STICK STICKERS:** Yes! Use them! And stamps, and the like! Students of all ages love them. Buy stickers when they are on sale after holidays and stockpile for future use.
- **COLOR:** Use colored pens of many shades. Students love it! The more unusual the color, the more of an attention grabber it is. For example, bright purple shrieks, "Look at what I have written on your work!" You can even color-code, perhaps marking math in red and science in green, or develop a special event code, maybe orange for Halloween, red for Christmas, and so on. The gold and silver flow pens now available everywhere are excellent for special assignments! Using many colored markers may sound frivolous, but students are more motivated to look over the marking if their interest is piqued.
- **GIVE CUES:** Use cues such as "see me" on work that requires further attention from you. Provide a specific time each day for students to see you one on one, and then initial the "see me" on their work. The initialling helps ensure that they meet you.
- **TEACH THROUGH MARKING:** Have students mark each other's work only if you can justify the activity as a learning experience.

For example, marking spelling where the marker is expected to write the correct spelling beside an error *may* meet this criterion. But for the most part, having students mark is only giving them busy work.

- **RECORD MARKS:** Only record marks in your permanent record if students have been prewarned; otherwise, they may not do their best work and you will probably alienate them instead. We know when our actions are being recorded, for example, you know when the superintendent will be visiting, and react accordingly. Give your students this same right!

- **REVIEW:** Always go over work, tests, and assignments with students after the work has been marked. For areas where all were successful, give yourself a pat on the back for a good job teaching that particular segment. Focus on areas commonly done incorrectly. While marking, keep a list of problem questions/areas for quick identification and later individual, small group or whole class instruction.

- **READ THE NAME LAST:** Look at the names on tests, etc., *after* marking them. In this way, you can avoid a predetermined expectancy for a particular student. Remember that we really do see what we want or expect to see.

Marking Creative Writing

Marking creative writing, whether it be a single sentence from a Grade 1 student or a five-page essay from a Junior High student, is always going to be highly subjective. The best you can do about this is to be consistent. Here are a few ideas that have proven useful to me.

- Always ask if students want you to mark directly on their finished copy. They may not. Getting back a piece of work on which hours have been spent, all marked up with red pen, is discouraging. There are several ways to handle the potential problem.
  a. Use a pencil and number areas of the paper worthy of positive comments or constructive criticism. Then add another piece of paper and write the comments, coded to the appropriate numbers.
  b. Use the little stick-on pads so that students can read your comments then remove them from their work if they so desire. Remember — the work belongs to them!

c. Ask students to hand work in in a clear duotang. You can then write with washable flow pen directly on the clear covering.

d. Write directly on the work with an erasable pencil and a light touch. The comments can later be erased!

- If, in a writing assignment, you are planning to evaluate *everything*, let students know ahead of time. Otherwise, if, for example, you are looking primarily for creative ideas, don't penalize for poor spelling. You may want to comment on the spelling, but don't deduct marks for it this time! Mark only what you say you are going to mark.

- Make use of a standard marking form such as you can find in most teachers' reference books or can create yourself. The form indicates how much value will be placed on each specific area. For example: under 40% allowed for grammar, sentences might be worth 10%; punctuation, 10%; capitalization, 10%; and spelling, 10%. Once you have a workable form, give students a copy of it before they begin writing. In this way, they know where to focus their efforts. The weighting on the form can change with specific assignments, for example, the value of grammar may be increased to 50% immediately after several lessons on it, but the basic form should remain the same.

- Always give specific suggestions for improvement. If a story ending is weak, for example, suggest how it could be improved or where the student could go for further help. Then — and this is the key — check back when marking the next piece of writing to see if your suggestions have been used.

- Have each student keep all final, marked copies of pieces of work in a separate binder or folder, so that you can check at any time for progress, and watch for action on suggestions, etc. I found that, by having a special basket in my room for these folders, the likelihood of students keeping their work together increases. Also, visiting parents, peers, and supervisors can gain ready access to the students' collective work. And you know where to turn when final evaluations must be made!

- Although providing percentage marks is difficult, and indeed, the most subjective part of marking writing, students appreciate them more than grade values, such as B –. You may find it appropriate to give two marks — one comparing the student's work to his/her previous work, and one comparing the work to the class mean. This double marking is time costly, so perhaps use it only for special assignments. And remember to convert irregular marks, such as 21/32, into percents. Even students who can do this for themselves appreciate seeing the actual percentage mark on their papers. Use a calculator. The converting only takes a minute, and what's one more minute when you have already spent hours marking? Naturally, the simplest route is to design a test out of 50 or 100, but as we all know, doing so seems easier to plan than to achieve.

- Personal comments specific to the particular piece of work are a must! What did you particularly like about it? How did this manuscript (even if it is just a couple of Grade 2 sentences) make you feel? Is there some aspect of the work you really appreciated? Students love to know your personal reactions which help them to appreciate the value of their work.

- If the work is well below your expectations for a particular student it's OK to say, "This is unacceptable. Please redo and hand in by ____." Always give students a second chance. They may choose to refuse it, but by offering it, you are promoting learning rather than punishment for poor work.

Also, be sure to check for any extenuating circumstances that may have affected this assignment. I once received a terrible piece of writing from a Junior High student whose work was usually excellent. Assuming that the student was "testing" or feeling lazy, I gave her a mark of 50 percent and didn't offer a second chance — the student was used to getting 80-90 percent. I later discovered that her father had passed away the day before the assignment was due. You can imagine my guilt! Don't assume! Check the situation out!

However, if you are not aware of extenuating circumstances until after you have given the low mark, explain your action, sincerely apologize for a lack of sensitivity or misunderstanding, if that is called for, then either offer the student a second chance at the assignment or agree to omit the low mark completely.

D. Writing and Administering Tests

A teacher must be a prophet who can look into the future, see the world of tomorrow, into which the children of today must fit, and then teach and test the necessary skills.

— *Anonymous*

Tests, unfortunately, are necessary evils. Used appropriately, they can be effective tools for diagnosis, record keeping, lesson planning, teacher self-evaluations, student progress evaluations and so on. Used incorrectly, they can be punitive and threatening. They should always be used with a specific reason in mind.

Creating a Better Test

Although educators often make use of standardized and norm-referenced tests, they more frequently rely on self-made, criterion-referenced tests. It is to these tests that the following points apply.

- Try, whenever possible, to test the application of skills and knowledge, not the rote recall of facts. We all know this, but can easily forget it. Here are two examples of meaningful scenarios:
  a. Testing a Health unit on First Aid: During an art class, a fellow student gets a cutting tool wedged into his hand. What would you do?
  b. Testing a Language Arts unit on Letter Writing: Write two letters about camp: one to your friend, and one to the company that sponsored the camp.
- Every test should include some questions that allow students to express opinions, to go beyond the mere recall of facts. Consequently, time must be allowed, posttest, for discussing differences of opinion. A good rule to follow is that a student should receive full credit for an answer if he or she can convince you of its merit.
- Make a permanent record of all test marks. Doing so shows that you consider tests to be important and increases student accountability, too. However, you do not have to use all the recorded marks when consolidating final grades — students needn't be aware of this.
- Always allow for retests, second chances which, if not provided, make tests punitive rather than learning tools. The entire subject of retesting is a touchy one with already overloaded teachers. But teachers are paid to teach, not just evaluate, and it's almost a certainty that students, on a second chance, will work hard to improve their marks. They will learn, and that's what it's all about! A retest should differ slightly from the original, although the content will be the same. And you may wish to put some condition on the retest. For example, the final test

re-tests!

mark may be an average between the two tests. No harm will come of allowing students second and even third chances. And if that seems like a lot, think of how many chances we, as teachers, get to teach again and again and again!

- Add little helps on tests, that is, any devices or techniques that allow students a breather from the concentrated effort required during a test. You might add a silly choice on a multiple choice question, add, half-way through, a very easy or obvious question, inject some humor into the test, or add a cartoon, happy face, sticker, even a frown face if it's a tough question, together with a brief phrase, such as Almost done or Hang in there, at various places throughout the test.
- If your students are Junior High, conclude a test with something such as this: "Write a question you wish had been asked on this test and then answer it correctly." Give marks for both the question and the answer. You offer the student a chance to show what he or she does know while practising a valid teaching technique. (You may also end up with some excellent questions for your next exam!)
- As a variation from the norm, provide students with the answers and ask them for the questions.

As a final note on test writing — create a test with a goal in mind. Know exactly what you are looking for. If it is just recall of some important facts or formulas, so be it. But if it is the application of skill, understanding and generalization, much more thought must be put into the creation of the test. Tests can be meaningful or time wasting — it's up to you!

Administering Tests

Tests cause anxiety in most students, but there are some things a teacher can do to help reduce such stress and thereby receive superior performances from the students.

- Before a test, teach students how to study. Study with them. First, make study sheets (handouts) from their notes, and go over them as a whole class. Then have them make study sheets in small groups or pairs, after pointing out a few of the key points for them, and let them review together.

  Eventually, you can ask them to make their own study sheets as a class assignment (worth marks of course). In this way, you are shaping their behavior so that eventually they will feel confident studying on their own. How many times have you heard, "I don't know how to study!" So teach them how. Good teaching is helping the student to get along without you, and that's exactly what you will be doing. Share any little study tricks you, yourself, have used. Here are a few possibilities:

a. Work out patterns for memorization of difficult and important facts. My Grade 6 class came up with the following sentence to memorize the order of the planets, adding the last word for the sake of the sentence's sense: My Very Entertaining Mother Just Smiles Until No Problems remain. This technique of association between the familiar and the unfamiliar can be taught with amazing results.

b. Create humor where there is none. For example, when teaching students that decimals always round up rather than down, compare decimals to a herd of cattle: both can be "rounded up." Turn to pun books for ideas.

• Teach relaxation exercises to be used pretest and even during the test if necessary. Students will perform much better if they can lose some tension; some students approach every test as if it were a life-and-death matter. Suggest and practise, pretest, techniques such as these:

a. Spend 30 seconds in absolute silence to have students compose themselves by concentrating, eyes closed, on a peaceful place, thing, or person.

b. Practise slow, controlled breathing, where each breath is counted, for one or two minutes.

c. Take a few seconds to shut the eyes and concentrate on something such as the heart beating, the sound of the furnace, etc.

d. Play a soothing piece of music for your students, or read a short, appropriate poem. The music works well with younger students; the poetry, with Junior High students.

e. Enjoy an appropriate cartoon on the overhead (keep a file of such cartoons).

f. Taking a couple of minutes for progressive muscle tensing and relaxing seems to help many students, too. Simply ask them to relax, then, keeping your voice quiet and level, ask them to alternately tense, hold for five seconds, then relax specific muscles or body parts. Scrunching up the eyebrows is particularly good!

Many excellent tapes and ideas for relaxation are available. Check the local library and music store for some that may be useful to you and your students. My favorite is "Trade Wind Island," a tape of ocean and sea gull sounds that Junior High students love and even request before a difficult test. The tape is part of Dan Gibson's series, *Solitudes* (produced by Holborne Distributing).

- At the beginning of an important test, I sometimes give out good-luck treats, for example, a Smartie to each student, a star stamped on the back of their hands so that they will be stars, or even a special pencil. Junior High students who usually write three or four large end-of-term exams in a row love the pencils. Such gimmicks may seem frivolous to you, but to the students they are indicators that you care, and I have never had a student of any age refuse one. Once, one of my Junior High students refused to wash his hand until after three days of exams were over, because he was "saving" the star stamps I was providing before each test! Shaking the hand of each student and wishing him or her good luck works too!

- Don't disappear while students are writing an exam, either by leaving the room or hiding behind a pile of papers or books. Circulate quietly and be visible! By doing so, you reinforce the importance you are placing on the test and give the students silent support. A smile or a pat on the back when a student is looking particularly frustrated can be very encouraging. I know that it is tempting to breathe a sigh of relief and sit down to relax when students are writing an exam, but your role during the writing of the exam is just as important as the students'. They *need* you there in body as well as spirit!

- Keep in mind that some students' difficulties in reading will adversely affect their test writing in all areas, and don't penalize them for this. Have a buddy (older student, aide, parent) read the questions to the student. In today's world, some of us may never be good readers, but that will not prevent excellence in other areas.

- Use the pre/post test technique, where exactly the same test is given twice. Either give it to the students to take home and study from, or give it two days in a row, recording only the second mark. "But," you say, "that's cheating. They will know exactly what to study and they won't study anything else." Well, as you probably already know, most students won't study anyway! And those that do, have as much chance of studying less important areas as important ones. If you *really* want them to learn specific material, give them the test *twice*. Doing so almost guarantees that students will study and learn. You can adopt this idea for basic factual recall areas, eg., math formula recall, or for opinion essay or long-answer questions where the students need to know specific material before they can state their opinions. Naturally, don't plan to use this technique exclusively, but try it once in a while. You'll like it and so will your students.

- Return tests as soon as possible after they have been written. (The younger the student, the more important it is to do this.) And don't forget to allow time to discuss at least some parts of the test thoroughly.
- Keep in mind that tests will be more valid and meaningful if evenly distributed throughout the term; also, more, smaller tests give students a better chance than few, lengthy ones. If you make one test too difficult, you can make it up next time around!

Remember: Writing a creative test, and marking a test creatively are vital teaching skills not to be taken lightly. Also, what you are testing at any given moment is only one small part of the whole child's knowledge, so neither success nor failure should be overemphasized.

E. Reporting and Report Cards

> What we want to see is the child in pursuit of knowledge, not knowledge in pursuit of the child.
> — *George Bernard Shaw*

Everyone seems to hate report card time. Teachers hate it because they must make sometimes very difficult decisions about students and spend hours of extra work. Students hate it because they are afraid the results will not be ''good enough,'' and parents hate it because they may have to take a stand with their children or children's teachers if the results are unsatisfactory. But reporting is necessary, and it doesn't have to be negative. Let's examine some ways to lessen the load.

- Never wait until report card time for either good or bad news. Make a habit of regularly phoning, sending home happy grams or notes, etc. Some parents are very accessible and passing on a good word to them is easy; others are almost invisible. Strive to contact parents regularly. The only way to achieve this is to set aside a specific time (10 min/week is enough) and do it!

- Begin the year with a letter to parents outlining your individual program, expectations, etc. If possible, note some of the areas you will be studying. For example: "In Science we will cover units on Magnets, Rocks and Minerals, Scientific Methods and Ecosystems."

- At about Christmas, send home a letter briefly outlining areas already covered. Parents appreciate knowing what is going on (we all know that when a parent asks a child what he or she learned at school that day the proverbial response is "nothing"!) and the summary keeps you accountable to yourself. Send home a similar review in the spring.

- When you must report something negative, be prepared to offer a possible solution. Explain what you expect of the parents and of the child. Also, say what *you* are going to do about the situation. Never leave parents with a problem that they have no idea how to solve. Example:

    Johnnie is very creative, but has difficulty in organizing his ideas to put them on paper. (**SPECIFIC INFORMATION AS TO THE PROBLEM**) *Consequently, he becomes frustrated and refuses to write at all.* (**SPECIFIC BEHAVIORS NOTICED**) *He should list the events he wants to put in his story, then, with your help, put them in the correct order before he begins to write. Get him to tell you his story aloud first.* (**EXACTLY WHAT YOU WANT THE PARENTS TO DO**) *I will give him extra help at noon on Wednesdays to be sure he is going in the right direction, and I'll let you know if he needs additional guidance.* (**EXACTLY WHAT YOU WILL DO**)

- If you don't have any solution to an existing problem, don't dump it all on the parent. Ask for parental input and suggestions, then offer to seek help elsewhere if necessary. Be positive. Never indicate that you are giving up! Example:

    Sally is having a lot of trouble getting along on the playground. She tends to be very rough with the smaller children, and although I have spoken to her several times, the behavior continues. (**SPECIFIC PROBLEM CLEARLY STATED**) *I wonder if you've noticed any behavior like this at home, or if you have any suggestions on how to deal with it...* (**ASKING FOR PARENTAL INPUT**) *I would like your permission to get* *some advice about this from* _____. (SEEKING HELP ELSEWHERE AND STATING EXACTLY WHAT YOU WILL DO) *Could you come in to see me on* _____? (EXACTLY WHAT YOU WANT PARENTS TO DO)

- Be sure to keep copies of all letters to/from parents, and to document carefully all visits, conferences, phone calls and the like. Invariably, you'll need the one piece of correspondence you've discarded or the date of a specific phone call. Be prepared! File it now!
- Let parents know early in the year when they can get in touch with you. If you don't provide a specific time, for example, Mondays, 3 p.m. to 4 p.m., then you will be getting calls and visits at the most inopportune times. Make yourself approachable. You are both on the same side.

Report Cards

Today there are as many different types of report cards as there are ways of reporting progress, but there are still some common factors to keep in mind.

- Report honestly. If you give every child high marks and glowing comments, all you are doing is to make yourself look effective and thereby avoid confrontation with unhappy parents or administrators. Of course, acknowledge the areas where each child excels. Also, there are times and instances where the self-esteem of a particular child is at stake and you should "juggle" marks. But giving consistent, unwarranted good marks is just avoiding responsibility. If a student is failing a subject, say so. Then take the necessary action to change this situation. The effects of dishonest reporting are far-reaching and cannot be overestimated. Not only does the student either get a false self-image or loss of confidence in the integrity of the teacher and educational system, but next year's teacher has to deal with parents and students faced with unexplainable mark drops. Marking and reporting honestly and objectively are essential.
- Focus on communicating clearly. Don't try to impress parents with your knowledge of educational jargon. Instead of talking mysteriously about "regrouping," use the more familiar term "borrowing". Rather than "whole language," talk about "stories written by the children themselves." Be careful not to make parents feel foolish just because they may not know what an integer, ecosystem, or intransitive verb is.

- Be specific, not syrupy, over-complimentary, or vague. Instead of "Bob is a wonderful boy," write "Bob has a great sense of humor and is very considerate of others."
- Acknowledge every child's strengths and weaknesses. Sometimes finding something really positive to say about a particular student who has been driving you crazy is difficult; if you find this, put the report card away until another time and try again, using one of those wonderful sets of possible comments available everywhere. If you can't find one, start your own and keep it handy during report card time. Also, remember that even the best students have areas on which additional work could be done.
- Write your report cards early! Last minute, hurried reports tend to reflect the lack of consideration they are given and are unfair to both students and parents. Plan to do just a few at a time. You will be less likely to say exactly the same thing about each student. Think about what you are saying, then reread what you have written.
- Be careful when using computer-coded remarks. A simple error in filling in those tiresome little bubbles can result in a ridiculous remark. For example, I accidentally put "muscular development is below what is expected for his age" (a Physical Education remark) under Sex Education. I never got any feedback, but I really wonder what the boy's parents thought I meant.
- Photocopy reports if you don't have a carbon copy. (Don't rely on getting them back!) Then, when writing second or third reports, refer back to the previous one(s) to seek changes (positive or negative), and to avoid contradicting yourself. Doing this also prevents using either exactly the same, or opposite comments on consecutive reports which can be quite embarrassing.
- Write or print neatly! Only doctors can get away with illegible writing. If yours is terrible, either get someone else to do it for you while you dictate, or type. Use perfect grammar and spelling. A teacher is a model always!
- Although putting percentage averages on report cards is not usually necessary for elementary school, it is necessary for Junior High. Find and familiarize yourself with a good computer marks program.
- Utilize both individual achievement and norm-referenced

achievement. Indicate the student's individual improvement, but don't neglect to say how he/she compares to the norm. Be especially careful to do this in Special Education, where the student may have made significant gains, but still be functioning well below what is expected for his or her chronological age. If the report merely indicates the gains, the parents (and student) can be seriously misled. Here is an example of one way with which to deal with the problem:

> *Joey has really improved in his reading. He has completed three levels since the last report, and now reads fluently on his own. He is now reading at a mid-grade 2 level, only one year behind what is considered average for his age. He has worked hard to close this gap and should be proud of his achievements.*

- This point may seem silly, but don't bribe or threaten students with upcoming report cards. Resist any temptation to say, "Stop that or it will go on your report card!" or "You'd better be good today because I'm writing report cards tonight." Have you heard that before? I must admit that I have, in jest of course, been known to say, "Hey guys, I'm writing report cards tonight. Anyone want to sweep the snow off my car after school?"
- Be aware that you can obtain printouts of every possible comment you'll ever need for a report card. Although these can be useful if you know what you want to say but can't find the right words, they have built-in pitfalls. For instance, it's too easy to pick the phrase first then fit it to some unsuspecting child. This backwards approach results in rather meaningless, non-specific reporting. Think of the child and what you want to report, then put the idea in your own words.
- Remember that when you write a report, you are creating a lasting document of that child's strengths and weaknesses. Choose your words wisely. Complete the report card with extreme care.

F. Conducting Parent-Teacher Conferences

> Parents are the bows from which their children,
> as living arrows, are sent forth.
> — *Kahlil Gibran*

The subject of how to effectively handle a conference with parents has surely suffered from overkill in teachers' handbooks, so it will be dealt with briefly. Among numerous ideas, a few stand out.

- Be prepared. Plan for the conference just as you would plan a good lesson. Work out how you will establish rapport and focus attention, what specific areas you wish to discuss and why, what information you will leave the parent(s) with, and how you will summarize the meeting for them.
- Decide ahead of time exactly what the purpose of the conference is. Is it just information sharing? Is it a "pat on the back" for diligent parents and students? Or is it information seeking in an attempt to handle a specific problem?
- Have all material on hand, including the student's marks, work samples (provide samples of other students' work if a comparison is necessary), texts being used, and homework checklist. (See the Parent-Teacher Conference form.)
- Allow 15 min for a conference and stick to it. The exception is where a parent specifically requests a longer meeting. If, at the end of the 15 min, you can see that no satisfactory closure can be made at that time, arrange another conference, and keep to your schedule. Let the parent(s) know at the outset exactly how much time you have.
- Write down questions you wish to ask or information you want to share. Don't rely on your memory.
- Dress appropriately. If you have just come from the gym in a sweatsuit, take time to change. First impressions are lasting, and parents' impressions of you will be handed down to their children.
- Arrange chairs of equal, adult size, so that parents are meeting you as equals. (Consider how parents must feel when the teacher talks from behind the shield of a desk, and they are squashed into tiny desks.)
- Be sensitive to single-parent families, adoptive parents, and children from foster or group homes. Be sure you know who these students are ahead of time, as well as the names of the supervisory adults.
- Remember that parents are anxious, even more so than you are. You are in control, so begin, and end, with a smile. Try to make them feel at ease by knowing their names, their child's name, etc. Shake hands when you meet (unless you know them well, in which case, doing so may seem silly and formal). And

send letter home w/ ?s re: seating Frustr

PARENT-TEACHER CONFERENCE

Student _____

Parent(s) _____

Positive statement _____

_____

Problem area _____

_____

Teacher's suggestions for dealing with this problem

_____

_____

CHECKLIST OF ITEMS TO HAVE AVAILABLE:

1. Student's marks _____

2. Samples of student's work _____

3. Samples of other students' work if a comparison is

   desirable _____

4. Log of inappropriate behaviors, dates provided, if behaviors

   are to be discussed _____

5. School priorities, rules, calendar, and manual _____

6. Curriculum outlines _____

7. Examples of books used _____

8. Appropriate seating arrangements _____

---

begin with some small talk to break the ice; however, some parents would rather get right to the heart of the matter, so evaluate the situation quickly and decide which tactic will be best. Don't wait for the parents to lead off. That is your responsibility!

- Be prepared for the inevitable "How is _____ doing?" This question seems to be the way most parents open their part of the conversation. So have an answer ready that is both positive and focusing, that is, leading the discussion where you want it to go. For example: "Carrie is doing well academically, but

I'm concerned about the problems she is having in socializing. Specifically, she seems to...."

- Never present a problem without explaining how you have been trying to deal with it or will try to deal with it. Also, be sure to suggest what the parents might try at home and ask them for suggestions. If you are both really stuck, be prepared to suggest other avenues of help. Have these checked out with your principal before the conference, so that you can speak with authority and let the parents know that something will be done. Never leave parents with a school-related problem to solve all on their own. It is your problem too.

- Listen carefully to what parents are saying, and clarify statements if you are unsure as to their meaning. Be sure you know exactly what the parents expect of you. If their expectations are unrealistic, say so, and explain why. Every once in a while, and especially at the end, summarize key points for the parents and yourself.

- Be supportive! Parenting is very difficult and any teacher who blames a parent for a child's problem has probably not been a parent. In any given case, intervening variables exist, and parents are usually doing the best they can do. Perhaps they believe a problem is all the teacher's fault, and we know that can't be true! Everyone involved is equally responsible — you are in this together.

- Be prepared to accept responsibility for the student's learning, or lack thereof, at school. Every student can learn. As the trained professional, you are being paid to find and implement the method that will expedite this learning. The parents can offer suggestions, but the responsibility is yours alone.

- Similarly, do not delegate your responsibility to the parents. When you place them in the role of teacher, for example, by assigning homework that requires more than just general supervision, you are creating an unnatural situation which is usually nonproductive and even harmful to the parent/child relationship. Parents cannot teach school curriculum to their children for two reasons: the children do not see them as teachers and the parents are unfamiliar with the requirements of the curriculum.

What you can and should expect parents to do, is to provide a consistent time and place for homework, together with appropriate consequences for its completion. The rest is up to you!

- Be aware of your body language during an interview. Do you constantly look at your watch? Do you maintain eye contact? If you are unfamiliar with the importance of body language, obtain a book such as *Body Language* by Julius Fast (1970) and learn more about the subject.
- End on a positive note, and leave an open invitation for them to contact you. Thank them for coming.
- If you are unfortunate enough to meet a hostile parent, let him (it's usually a father) talk. Listen quietly and ask him specifically what is wrong. Then calmly restate the situation in your own words, adding your concerns, and go from there. Remain calm at all times! If the situation is completely impossible, close the conversation and suggest another time for the interview.
- Consider the possibility of having the student sit in on the interview and participate. Some teachers don't feel comfortable doing this, and of course you must do what is right for you, but the presence of the student can promote honest, open communication and concern.
- As soon as possible after a conference, jot down a few notes about it. Did you meet your objective? Did the parent(s) understand your concerns? Were possible solutions suggested? Was a follow-up conference date arranged? What are your responsibilities as a result of the conference?
- Don't overlook or underestimate the importance of the physical appearance of your classroom during a conference. Shelves, boards, bulletin bords, and desks all make a statement about you.

Teaching today's youth is not done in isolation. Teachers are not the only ones who influence children, and we must always remember that we are in partnership with parents, guardians and any other significant adults in the students' lives. So, let us not be vain about our roles — important though they may be. Young people come to respect, learn and master skills introduced and taught by a variety of individuals.

CHAPTER 4

Relating

A. Relating to Students as Children

TEACHER: (to surly child who has been acting up) Trevor, I
    don't know what to do with you, I don't know what to do
    for you. What is it *you* want me to do?
STUDENT: (spitting out the words) How should I know? You're
    the teacher!
TEACHER: (spontaneously) Well, how about a hug then?
STUDENT: (first surprised, then throwing his arms around
    teacher's neck) Thanks!

The teacher in this scene was me, and the incident marked the
beginning of hug therapy where, if a student was having a bad
day, he or she could say so, and readily receive a big hug from
the teacher. This form of intervention was, of course, controver-
sial, but it worked for me.

But other than hugs, how should we respond to students' private problems, especially those that have an impact on the whole
classroom? I have urged you to get to know the whole child, so
what, if anything, should you do if you see a child in some sort
of crisis or negative situation? Every teacher is very aware of the
fine line between becoming involved and becoming over-involved
with students, but when it comes to a child or adolescent in obvious need, each teacher must make an individual choice about
the depth of that involvement. You must acknowledge and report
any suspicious incidents and arrange for some sort of intervention or counselling for the student. Beyond this, the limits of
involvement are purely personal.

I am notorious for becoming too involved, but I do not plan
to change. I believe firmly that a truly caring teacher can help.
Often, just showing genuine concern is enough to see a troubled
youth through a crisis. However, becoming involved is dangerous

and not for everyone. It carries with it the risk of the teacher being totally overwhelmed by students' problems and suffering much personal stress. Teachers who have complex personal lives and many demands on them outside of teaching cannot be expected to become involved with children in crisis willingly, once their legal and professional duties have been met. Again, the parameters that a teacher sets for involvement with students are strictly personal; there is no right or wrong.

The purpose of this section is not to delve into the causes and cures of the many crises facing today's youth, but rather, to examine some ways in which any teacher can respond to a child in some crisis or difficulty.

- **THE HUNGRY CHILD:** Provide a snack for the whole class at the beginning of both the morning and the afternoon. Funds for this can be earned as a class project, collected from parents, or possibly taken from the school budget. Or, contact Social Services and tell the department about the student. Another option is that you, yourself, can provide the individual with nourishment. Most schools will allocate some funds for this. I fed several very hungry teenagers a few years ago and the cost was my own, but I never regretted doing so.
- **THE CHILD CAUGHT IN A CUSTODY BATTLE:** Be alert to mood swings, and be prepared to quietly remove the child from class if you suspect an outbreak of emotion. Give the child sincere empathy; tell him or her that you are available to talk at any time, but do not try to force the child to see you. With older students, have them write down all their feelings, thoughts, and reactions about what is happening. Assure them of confidentiality. And keep aware of the situation. If the child has to move, be especially caring. I took a teenage girl out for lunch on the day of the actual separation of her parents. Although she didn't eat much, she did cry a lot, and I think she felt better for it.
- **THE CHILD WHO MIGHT BE ABUSED:** Be aware of your legal responsibility to report any suspicions of abuse to authorities, beginning with your school principal. Be aware of school board policy on reporting possible abuse — policy differs between boards. Don't attempt to hug or touch a possibly abused child unless he or she initiates the contact. Usually, an abused child is frightened by contact of any sort. And don't try to encourage

the child to explain injuries or bruises. Rather, let the child know that you care and are available if he or she ever wants to talk.

- **THE CHILD AFFECTED BY A FAMILY OR NEIGHBORHOOD TRAGEDY:** The tragedy might be a death in the family, a local kidnapping or exposure to violence. If it is a neighborhood tragedy, several of the students may be aware of the situation, and so a group discussion may be of value. Sometimes, talking with peers can be more helpful than talking with adults. If just one child appears to be affected, however, ask the child's permission to discuss the situation with the class, and honor his/her decision. One-on-one discussions can also be helpful, as long as you feel comfortable with the situation. As previously suggested, have older students write down all their thoughts and concerns; you can then write back and address some of the concerns. Finally, if your school or board has a crisis management team, be sure to refer any child affected by a tragedy to it for counselling.

- **THE PICKED-ON CHILD:** Teaching a few assertive behaviors and comebacks can be helpful here. I once taught a child who was constantly being picked on by others to say, ''That hurt!'' when a peer would call her a name. If the peer then responded with ''Good, it was supposed to,'' the child would then reply, ''Well, it did!'' Then the girl was to turn and walk away, having had the last word, so to speak. I'm happy to report that the strategy worked beautifully. The child who was dishing out the putdowns was so startled that she, as well as others, soon stopped. In addition to trying to teach a picked-on child to be assertive, do what you can to improve the child's self-esteem, which is probably low. Being able to do so will often reduce the intimidation by peers.

Remember, the role of the teacher is one of helper — not just in the area of curriculum learning, but in day-to-day living. As an individual, you will have to decide on the degree of your involvement with your students, but total lack of involvement is impossible. After all, if you didn't want to be involved with young people, you wouldn't be a teacher!

B. Lightening Up in the Classroom

Laughter really is the best medicine, but the taking of medicine is a reactive measure — an attempted cure. You can use laughter actively to help prevent ills such as stress and fatigue in your students and yourself.

Laughter is the classic way of lightening up. And you need to lighten up, to relax and take all that life throws at you less emotionally. In other words, try to remain *calm*! "How can I possibly be calm when Michael is hitting Shelly, Simon is eating chalk, all the girls are giggling and the principal is at the door?" you ask. Well, obviously there are times when being calm is out of the question, and perhaps a better motto might be "when all else fails — scream!" But in the general everyday hustle and bustle and stress of teaching, you can take a few measures to lighten up. Here a few pieces of advice that I hope will be helpful.

- Check students' perceptions of situations before reacting. Perhaps what you took to be an insult was intended to be a joke. Perhaps what you thought was a smart-alec answer was an unsuccessful attempt at humor.

- Don't embarrass one student in order to create humor for the others. I once presented a Grade 6 student, who always seemed to have something such as a pencil, comb or eraser in his mouth, with a baby's pacifier in front of the whole class. The class laughed, but the student felt humiliated and I was mortified. Remember that the self-esteem of children is fragile!

- Keep rules to a minimum and lighten up on discipline. It's annoying, frustrating, and upsetting when a student misbehaves, but putting that student on the spot or creating another such stressful situation for him or her will not prevent the same thing from happening again. On the other hand, handling misbehavior with a lighter touch might lessen the stress for both of you. Sometimes laughing at a problem can diffuse a potentially dangerous power struggle. When we consider some of the truly terrible problems we could face with students, for example, drugs or gang wars, suddenly the problem of gum chewing does not seem so bad. Let's not overreact to minor behavioral lapses.

- Teachers often get angry at situations which students think are funny. Perhaps we should take a hint from our students and at least try to see the humor before reacting negatively. An example that comes to mind is that of the child who falls out of his desk, causing much laughter and confusion. Assuming, of course, that the student is not hurt, you could get angry and reprimand the student for his distraction of the class, or you could laugh briefly with the others, compliment the student on his performance (without embarrassing him), and then restore order. You should then explain why you don't want a repeat performance and indicate what the consequences of such an act would be. By choosing the latter response, you will have shared a humorous moment with the class (rather than have it taken away from you), and also have maintained control. I guarantee that everyone will feel better with this lighter approach.

- Remind yourself that teaching is more than a profession — it is a way of life! So take the easy way out of a precarious situation, and laugh! Get a realistic perspective! You aren't the centre of the universe, or even the first person to which something unfair has happened. If you have a realistic perspective, you will be able to take yourself lightly, even though you may be taking your job seriously.
- Let others know how you are feeling. If today is not a day for jokes, tell your students. They'll understand.

Remember humor is an attitude; it is a sense of joy in being alive. Share that with your students whenever you can.

C. Lightening Up in the Staffroom

The staffroom is the place where the tension of the classroom is carried and concentrated, where the frustration that can find no outlet in the classroom can explode and where teachers say and do things they don't necessarily mean and will probably regret later.

From years of experience I have deduced that the staffroom will always be a place to air complaints. And that is not necessarily bad. Difficulties shared are often difficulties lessened. The teachers who are more inclined to hide their emotions are the teachers who end up with stomachs that keep score!

But you can and should help to create a more positive atmosphere in the staffroom. Doing so takes a conscious effort, but if you care about the students (which you do or you wouldn't be reading this book), then you care about keeping your peers happy. As you already know, the happiness of the teacher has a direct impact on the happiness of the students.

- Make a Quotables Board: Simply laminate a colored piece of paper onto which you can tape interesting and particularly funny quotations or jokes. Change them as often as possible. The background board can be color-coded for the season with accompanying pictures if you are so inclined. Start keeping a file immediately and you will soon have it filled.
- Occasionally pop little surprises (anonymously) into all teachers' mailboxes (e.g., Easter eggs, candy canes, and wrapped chocolates).
- Make a Caught in Action Board on which you post humorous photos of staff at work or play. You can start it by giving a loaded camera to students or doing the rounds yourself. Teachers can be asked to participate by having an assigned month in which they are responsible for taking photos of peers. It can be a lot of fun. Favorites can even be shared with students, although this display is really for teachers only.
- Encourage potluck lunches; shared desserts; soup days; McDonald's Days, etc. Shared "fun" lunches are relaxing and well worth the slight inconvenience.
- Make it a point to remember teachers' birthdays. Get a list from the principal and buy a lot of cards at one time. Write them all at once if you like, mark the dates on your home and school calendars, and pop the cards into mailboxes.
- Every staffroom has a table cluttered with teachers' books — great idea! But here's another one! Add a few joke books (*The Far Side* is a good example) or humorous teacher books such as *Teachers: A Survival Guide for the Grownup in the Classroom* by Art Peterson and available, with other similar books, at most large bookstores. It's OK for teachers to take a break from curriculum, and have a chuckle or two. Making reading material such as this readily available helps to encourage this.
- Always have your eyes open for humorous calendars or posters related to school, children and teaching. They are an amusing addition to any staffroom. If you check the card stores in January, old calendars are usually half-price, but the pictures are just as funny. Cutting them out and making a Humor Board in the staffroom could be a task assigned to a student if you are too bogged down to do it.
- Splurge and buy a balloon arrangement for the staffroom table. Such an arrangement can be comical if you so request and lasts much longer than flowers.

- Place a large Coin Jar on the staffroom table. It can be just for loose change (those heavy little coins of relatively minor worth that weigh down your pockets) or for little fines (e.g., caught not washing out coffee cup — a common teacher fault!; missing a supervision; or being late for a staff meeting). The small change will accumulate quickly into a reasonable amount which can then be used for a special treat.
- Give the valuable gift of time. When you find yourself with 10 min you can spare (you'll have to make it, because teachers never really have 10 min to spare!), offer it to someone who seems really bogged down, a little discouraged, or even just in the midst of One of Those days. Make your offer hard to refuse. "I've got 10 min and I really want to do something for you. What will it be?" You might look out for opportunities to help with the following:
  a. marking
  b. recording marks
  c. manning the phones for the secretary (Don't forget the secretary and custodial staff. They are even more important to the school atmosphere than the teachers!)
  d. relieving a colleague in the classroom, that is, babysitting the class, to allow the teacher a little unexpected break
  e. sweeping snow off someone's car
  f. bringing a daily attendance record up-to-date
  g. photocopying
  h. putting work up on display

  Be sure you have a few ideas before offering a peer 10 min, because chances are he/she will immediately refuse. But if you make a specific suggestion, you will be taken seriously, and believe me, you'll both feel better when you give assistance.
- Try to encourage the staff, or as many of them as are willing, to occasionally entertain the students as a whole. For instance, they could "lip sync" a popular song or golden oldie at an assembly. Or they could improvise a little skit or play, for example, a well-known tale such as The Three Little Pigs. Dress accordingly, assign roles against type, for example, make the petite elderly teacher the Big Bad Wolf, and wing it. The students love this, and once the teachers are convinced to give it a try, they thoroughly enjoy it too.
- Become aware of your own staffroom face. Instead of blasting through the staffroom door, as is commonly the case, pause

briefly at the entrance, and relax the muscles of your face. I did an informal study of teachers coming into staffrooms and confirmed that most of us are scowling, frowning, or looking distressed in some way. And why not? Most likely the unhappy face reflects what the teacher has just gone through. Nonetheless, even if you have just fought with your entire class for 45 min, you can at least remove the scowl. If you make a conscious effort to do this, others will, too — with obvious results. Smiles are contagious — but so are frowns!

D. Practising Professionalism

There is much more to being a professional teacher than these few words would imply. Unfortunately, all too often the stresses and frustrations inherent in teaching batter our professionalism and obscure our best reasons for becoming teachers. We must strive to retain our sense of professionalism and to practise professional behavior. Here are some ways of doing this.

- Always attend several conferences, courses, in-services and other such professional development opportunities annually. (It often seems that the longer we have been teaching, the less we feel we need such stimulation; the opposite is true!) Keep a detailed record of what you attend. You are responsible for constantly upgrading your education and staying abreast of the latest innovations in the teaching field.
- Subscribe to and read an educational journal of your choice. There are many from which to choose. Select one that your school doesn't already have a subscription to.
- Change your established teaching units every year. Just because you have created or discovered a successful unit doesn't mean you should stop there. Changing units forces you to be creative and to update your resources and ideas, making your teaching more interesting and your students more interested.
- Be punctual, not only for work in the mornings, but for all school functions.
- Be dependable! Don't make promises you can't possibly keep, or commitments which, although your intentions were good, will become more than you can handle. Don't try to do too much, but do your share of extra jobs such as coaching and supervising dances. Know your limitations and work within them.

- Respect the confidentiality of students, parents, and peers. In teaching, perhaps more than in any other profession, many secrets come to your ears. If you suspect that a particular secret is one that you will, for legal reasons, be unable to keep, tell the student ahead of time. If, after hearing the secret, you can think of a way to help the student by involving others, ask permission to share the secret and explain why you want to do so. But otherwise, keep the secret!
- Take available sick time only when you really need to. Most school boards are generous and trusting with the allocation of casual sick time for their teachers, because they realize that teaching is demanding, exhausting and stressful. However, if you find it necessary to take regular rest and recreation breaks, perhaps you are in the wrong profession.
- Plan for every day! Although a good teacher can "wing it" sometimes, adequate lesson planning is an integral part of the profession. Without it, disorganization sets in, leading to less teaching and less learning!
- Accept, without complaining, your mundane staffroom duties. Nobody likes staffroom clean-up, lunchroom, recess or detention supervision, and staff meeting participation, but you and your peers have these responsibilities. Don't shirk them; do your part.
- The next time you feel like voicing a complaint, think of something else instead. Think positively. Smile. You may even make yourself feel better in the process.

Practising professionalism is easier to talk about than to do, but every teacher must try to do it. If you view your students not as an unruly class, but as the generation of tomorrow, if you understand and appreciate the importance of your role of teacher, and if you accept the challenge of working with young people, then you will be well on your way to professional behavior. You must also strive actively to behave professionally — perhaps, it is in the striving for professionalism that we show that we are, indeed, professionals!

CHAPTER 5

Presenting

Every teacher has an affinity for art, interior design and stage direction, or he or she wouldn't be a teacher! This strength may be hidden beneath a million other more obvious talents, but trust me — it's there! The trick is to draw out those talents when necessary. I hope a few of the hints in this chapter will help you to do this.

A. Bulletin Boards

A bare room is like a boring teacher. Both lack the pizzazz which is the soul of learning.

Numerous books describe possible bulletin board displays, so the focus here will be on how to prepare a display rather than on what to do. As a rule, teachers are responsible for bulletin boards in their rooms, plus those adjacent to the rooms in the hall. Keeping these huge, imposing bleak boards interesting and current can seem an insurmountable task. Remember, however, these bulletin boards are an instant reflection of you and your class, so don't give up.

- Decide at the beginning of the year upon the function of each board for which you are responsible, and keep it consistent. For example, Bulletin Board (BB) #1 will represent the present Language Arts theme (see "Types of Boards"), BB #2, current events in/out school; and BB #3, samples of students' work.
- Put a colorful border around each board. A wide variety of pre-made borders are on the market, but they are expensive, and many other possibilities exist. A strip of newspaper makes a good current events border. Colored autumn leaves make an interesting students' work border in September. And anything related to the board theme works well, e.g., strings of paper

doll cutouts for a Kindergarten friendship theme. Borders are definitive and absolutely necessary for a finished look.

Types of Boards

- **THEME BOARD:** Whether you teach on a theme basis or simply follow the calendar year, there are always themes. I taught Language Arts using a monthly theme approach. At the beginning of each month (and each new theme), I prepared the theme board when students were not around. Seeing the board was an eagerly anticipated event for the students, who always wanted to know what we would be focusing on next.

   As you have probably done, you can also take themes or unit themes in specific core subject areas. For example, for a Science unit on ecosystems, you might do the following.

   Have a green, construction paper border. At the top of the board, place the word "ECOSYSTEMS"; in the centre, a poster showing any scene in nature such as a forest or pond. Using felt markers on construction paper, print key phrases such as "primary food source" and "secondary food source" and attach these to the display, with arrows pointing to the appropriate parts of the poster. Around the outside of the board, pictures of different animals that might be found in such a location, plus labels identifying their positions in the ecosystem, would finish off the display.

- **CURRENT EVENTS BOARD:** You might make this board the responsibility of the students, on a rotating basis. Birthdays, dances, and special days could be featured. Part of this board should be dedicated to news stories of interest to the students as well.

- **HALL BULLETIN BOARD:** Here is an opportunity to indicate to the rest of the school what your class is doing. Don't create the display in September and leave it until next June. Change it regularly. There are always samples of students' work worth sharing — just be sure to get their permission first!

No matter what the nature of the bulletin board, there are a few basic rules to keep in mind. Following these will not lessen the load of creating and putting up displays, but they might just help to relieve some of the anxiety often associated with this particular teacher task.

- Keep the display simple! Overcrowding is not eye-pleasing! Just because there are 30 students in your class does not mean there need be 30 samples of work. A few well-placed items, chosen according to merit or by rotation perhaps, will be viewed!

- Think of creative backgrounds that fit the particular display: for example, foil for a science fiction or space theme, white sheet or cotton batting or scattered cotton balls for a winter theme, orange paper or stretched cobwebs (available in card stores in October) for Halloween, sheer netting over a display for a fantasy theme, and a burlap background for a pioneer theme. Fabric, towels, curtains, sheets (flowered for spring) and the like all make interesting backgrounds which are different from the usual colored construction paper. And don't overlook the merits of the daily newspaper either. It can quickly cover a board before other items are mounted in a Current Events display or be cut into letters or shapes, such as palm trees for a holiday display. Best of all, it's cheap!
- Think of a snappy name for the display. Here are a few pointers on doing so.
  a. Use alliteration, for example, "Something Special" on a display of creative writing.
  b. Use or adapt words or phrases that students can relate to. For example, I once had a Mathmania display.
  c. Check through the daily newspaper for witty, eye-catching titles that can often be altered slightly to fit your display. For example, at my school, "Now Look Here, Pocklington" was changed to "Now Look Here, Crestwood!" on a pep rally display for a big game against Crestwood.
- Use three-dimensional materials wherever possible. Examples include candy canes and crackers on a Christmas display, paper-wrapped candies or ghosts made out of cheesecloth on a Halloween display, dry twigs, grass or wheat stalks on a fall display and colored yarn or ribbon (especially the curly ribbon) on any display to tie it all together. Straight pins, push pins and staples all attach items effectively. Tape will dry and fall off.
- Work samples need not be spaced in exact rows on the board. Overlapping can be interesting, as can random (collage type) placement; however, avoid this latter design with items you wish others to read, because doing so would be difficult.
- When at a loss for an idea, try an entire bulletin board of black and white silhouettes, perhaps of hands, flowers, people, or trees. If you choose a theme, for example, body parts for Health,

the design becomes more meaningful. However, sometimes a bulletin board can be created just for its entertainment value.

- Another snappy bulletin board is one made up of slogans or sayings directly related to education: "Teenagers' idea of a good book — something made into a TV movie," "If you think education is expensive — try ignorance," etc. Inexpensive books filled with such quotations abound and students love reading and illustrating them. Or, you can ask Junior High students to write their own sayings after a bit of guidance, thus creating a fun Language Arts lesson.

- Lettering for bulletin boards can be bought at any teachers' store but is quite expensive. Once you have a master, get students to cut letters from anything available — newspapers, grocery bags, gift wrap, computer paper, foil paper, wax paper, old magazines, newsprint, and old assignments (they love to cut up math assignments, for example, instead of just throwing them away). Lettering can also be done with wool, string, rope, straws, pipe cleaners, ribbon...the list is endless.

- Be sure to spell words correctly on any display. Mistakes show a lack of respect for both adults and students. If you have difficulty with this, ask a peer to check your board for you!

Remember that, although changing the bulletin boards may seem like a waste of your time, it's not! Attractive, effective bulletin boards are a powerful learning tool, as well as a reflection on your students and yourself. They give something to all who view them, be it a smile, a thought, a pat on the back or a piece of information. Make your bulletin boards special, and fit doing them into your busy schedule.

B. Displays

Great displays are 1 percent inspiration and 99 percent perspiration.

Here I am discussing the filling of those intimidating glass-front cabinets in eye-catching places in every school. Usually teachers take turns filling these cabinets, and pleading a lack of creative or artistic talent will not exclude you from this task. Don't panic. You, too, can create a wonderful display! Here are some pointers that I have found useful.

- Take the three glass shelves in the cabinet out and create your own levels, or, at the very least, levels on individual shelves. You can use large blocks from Kindergarten or Industrial Arts, stacks of books, or boxes and cover them with cloth or paper to create different levels in the cabinet. Working with levels is one of the first rules of creativity.

- Drape back and sides with cloth or cover with paper to fit the theme.
- Don't overcrowd! Here, again, less is better!
- Use thread to suspend items from the top of the cabinet. Keep the levels different!
- Name the display.
- Make sure the cabinet window is clean on both sides.
- When you want objects to stand up on their own, implant them in a small piece of clay or plasticine and then mask it.

Displays themselves can be of anything from classroom books to art projects to collections. I once saw a most interesting display of dolls and stuffed toys provided (on loan) by an elementary teacher's Grade 2 students. The other students spent hours gazing at this curious assortment of treasures, which took the teacher only a few moments to put together. Here are a few other examples of successful displays.

- For Christmas, you might do the following. Spray paint a dead tree branch silver or gold, and stand it in a lump of clay. Cover the clay base with cotton batting to create snow. Decorate the branch in any novel way such as with strings of popcorn and cranberries; homemade ornaments; origami birds; simple two-dimensional colored pictures, cut out and suspended by red curly ribbon; old jewelry (all those old earrings make wonderful decorations); curls of colored paper; and student-made snowflakes. Any small figurines fashioned by students from clay or plasticine or painted plaster of Paris ones (the unpainted ones are available at most craft and paint stores) can be arranged around the bottom of the branch, in a bed of "snow." Add a few wisps of angel hair and sprinkles of sparkle dust. Presto! Instant beauty!
- At the Junior High level, you could make candle centrepieces from half logs. To do so, collect fireplace wood and have a friendly parent or the Industrial Arts teacher split the wood for you and bore one hole in the centre for the candle. Glue on cones, decorations, clay characters, etc. White glue works

well but takes a long time to dry, so temporarily secure decorations with masking tape. Or choose a faster drying craft glue if you want to spend the money. Buy the cheapest red and green candles possible, and make a gift of one to each student. Once they get going, students can create wonderful centrepieces with materials they supply themselves.

Arrange the centrepieces around a mini-tree or a sprayed branch and add mini-lights that actually work! Amazing! Your students will feel like real wizards when they view this finished display, and of course they can take their centrepieces home for Christmas.

- Another Junior High Christmas diplay idea is to begin early in November with a clay project: have students make little houses, churches, people, Christmas trees, etc. Fire the clay once, then have students paint their projects and varnish them. Then you can create a winter scene in the display cabinet. First, remove any glass shelves and add your own levels covered with cotton batting for a snowy look. Add small branches standing in clay lumps as trees and a painted background (just sky and white hills will be enough). You will have a beautiful, winter postcard in the display cabinet!

- For Halloween, make jack-o'-lanterns out of several large pumpkins. Give the pumpkins names of staff (as long as the staff are notified and are willing) or amusing names. Add hats, hair of perhaps wool or grass, and a spiky background using dead branches, wheat shafts, dried leaves, etc. Cheesecloth draped around adds a ghostly appearance. The students love seeing their favorite teachers' names on comical pumpkins.

    NOTE: As the pumpkins will mould, this display will last only 7 to 10 days.

- You could also create a life-sized witch in the display cabinet by stuffing old black pants and a sweater with newspaper and adding gloves, boots, a full-head mask (also stuffed) and a hat. Position the witch so that she is holding a sign, a book or whatever. Instant success! You can even give her a name appropriate to your school, such as Crestwood's Crank.

- Celebrate spring. Create a blue background of paper or fabric and add a huge, painted rainbow. Suspend birds, butterflies and so on (made by students) from the top of the display case. Add huge tissue paper flowers to the base, using different levels as discussed earlier in this chapter.

- Mark Book Week. First, create several levels in the display cabinet. Seat a doll or stuffed toy holding a book on each level. Old reading glasses added to the toys' noses are effective. (Thanks to M. McRae for this idea.)
- For summer, you could create an underwater nook. First, cover the glass with green or blue netting or gauze, or clear elastic film or transparent tissue. Suspend colorful fish, each made of two flat fish attached and stuffed, from the top. Cover the bottom with shredded green crepe paper, curly ribbon, wrinkled tissue paper, and various sizes of rocks and shells. Hang strips of blue and green, curled curly-ribbon from the top.
- To feature color, choose any color and put items of only this color in the display. On the back wall of the cabinet, put excerpts from literature relevant to this particular color. For example, if you are featuring red, you could put a copy of Kathy Stinson's picture book, *Red Is Best*, in the cabinet. You could also add a little humor, for example, by adding a banana painted red. Brainstorm with your students for ideas.
- A varied collection makes an interesting and instant display for those times when you simply don't have the time to collect and be creative with students' work. Posters, especially of old examples of the following, make good backgrounds. Here are some all-occasion themes: hats, sports equipment, musical instruments, shoes and containers (students can be sent on a scavenger hunt for these).
- Generate student interest through a Guess Who display. Collect and mount baby pictures of staff members, but do not provide names. As a background, you could use large sheets of colored Bristol board, accordion-pleated so that photos can be mounted in an interesting way on each pleat.

You, too, can create a great display! Once the necessary materials have been collected, all it takes is about a half-hour of time. Keep an eye on store windows. Sometimes you can get an idea there that will lend itself to a school display. Some stores will even donate the ingredients of "old" displays to schools, and you can store possible display items. A variety of changing displays indicates a progressive, interesting school!

C. Concerts

> Children are not things to be molded, but people to
> be unfolded.
>
> — *G. F. Lieberman*

Planning for a school concert can provoke anxiety in even the
most creative teachers. Panic centres around the Question, "How
can I get everyone involved in some novel manner requiring a
minimum of sets, costumes and practice time?" Even when there
is one central theme for a school production (eg., Western Days),
each teacher must develop his or her own class's presentation.

Such presentations are subject to numerous limiting variables,
such as age and number of students, interests of students, poor
gym acoustics, limited practice time and teacher time. However,
since the school concert remains as inevitable as Christmas, here
are some tried and true suggestions that have been successful.

- **CLASS SONG OR CHORAL SPEECH:** Quite boring on its own, it
  can be spiced up with the addition of some of the following:
  a. A couple of students, suitably attired, mime the song/speech
     during the presentation.
  b. The entire group comes on carrying lighted candles and
     presents with the lights out.
  c. Some, or all, of the group carry flashlights. At a specific point
     in the presentation, house lights go off, flashlights go on,
     and students provide a light show by playing the lights on
     the ceiling. (Thanks to Pat Taylor.)
  d. Students first sing the song in normal fashion, then do it
     jazzed up to a funky rock beat, with accompanying move-
     ments. This approach works especially well if the song is
     a lullaby type. A Junior High variation is to present choral
     speech seriously, then as rap music.
  e. During the presentation, show transparencies depicting
     scenes relating to the song/speech on a large screen, or the
     wall, adjacent to the presenting group. Have the students
     use permanent felts on transparency film to prepare the pic-
     tures ahead of time.
  f. Students walk onto the stage, or, better yet, into the gym,
     carrying lighted sparklers as they sing. (Keep this idea for
     older students.)
  g. Every other student bobs up and down during each chorus;

when half are up, the other half are down and so on. Save this idea for a humorous presentation, because the incorrect bobbing that will inevitably occur is bound to spark laughter.

h. Students sing or speak through puppets that they have made, simple sock or paper bag puppets, or even elaborate paper mâché characters such as Junior High students love to create.

i. All students wear masks on sticks, perhaps depicting emotions related to the song/speech, characters or animals. The masks can be raised and lowered at appropriate times during the presentation. Naturally, the students themselves will have made the masks.

- **DANCING:** Getting students to dance may seem like a difficult task, but it is not impossible! And it is wonderful to behold an entire class dancing. The choreography should be very simple, for obvious reasons; you do not need to be a dancer to create a dance. You can try square dancing, line dancing, simple choreographed group dance, aerobic dance (borrow ideas from TV if necessary), and combination dancing, for example, jitterbug, ballroom dancing, and rap dancing all at once. Dancing works particularly well with Junior High students.

- **MARCHING:** This almost forgotten act can be very effective with young children or Special Education children who can easily be taught to march in simple patterns. A wide variety of marching music is available from libraries.

- **NARRATED STORY:** Any short story can be told, or read, by a narrator using a microphone, while others pantomime the sequence of events. This approach permits some acting while avoiding the problems that arise when students try to be heard in a huge gym.

- **GAME SHOW TAKE-OFF:** Take a TV game show as a model, change it slightly to fit your needs, and create a humorous parody of the original. Good shows to choose are ''The Price is Right'' and ''Jeopardy.''

- **CAPITALIZING ON THE COMPUTER ERA:** Any normal situation can be made hilarious if a robot makes mistakes.

a. A computerized robot teacher gives ridiculous directions to a Home Economics, Art or Physical Education class. Students try to follow the directions.

b. An entire class of robots can go astray and start doing everything wrong.

c. Working robots can be ordered to "dance," with a hilarious kick-line response.
- **THE TABLEAU TECHNIQUE:** Better suited to older students, this technique can be used in a variety of situations. Students freeze into positions that depict a specific scene (see following suggestions). When the curtain opens, the freeze is held either until the curtain closes again or until a predetermined point in the performance, at which time the scene comes alive. Students then move appropriately, dancing or pantomiming, until another cue causes them to freeze again. Several different tableaus can make up a very successful performance. The key is to have one or two narrators, using a microphone, to tie it all together. Here are some tableau suggestions: rock group with music; familiar fairy tales; poems, nursery rhymes, and songs; and commercials.
- **FAMOUS PERSONALITIES TAKE-OFF:** Older students especially like to imitate famous TV, movie or sports stars. Have some students improvise a scene in which the famous person and a student reporter meet by chance and discuss the school, the principal, or other people familiar to all.
- **NOW AND THEN COMPARISONS:** Using a narrator (or several narrators) describe situations from past and present as other students, appropriately dressed, come on and off stage and pantomime specific actions. For example, fitting in with the Social Studies theme of Pioneers, two examples of entertainment could be shared: pioneers playing a family game with homemade equipment; modern family members watching TV or playing computer games. The narration can be serious (pointing out some valuable information or even a moral) or humorous. For the finale, the people from the Past and Present could meet for a discussion, comparison...whatever. Possible scenarios are the following:
  a. Sports: A narrator describes a baseball game today, while a few students mime the action to the accompaniment of John Fogerty's song, "Centerfield." Then the narrator suggests what baseball might have been like in prehistoric days, while students mime a similar game using sticks and stones and end up hitting one another over the head. Accompanying music could be the theme from "The Flintstones."
  b. Dance: The narrator suggests that the rap dancers of today are not much different from the dancers of the past. Small

90

groups of students then come on and off demonstrating different dances in the order in which they occurred in history.

c. Music: The narrator introduces different types of bands, from past to present, and students mime playing the appropriate music. This activity is a favorite with Junior High.

The possibilities are limitless and students love creating the comparisons. They can also learn a lot by being asked to research the differences before creating the scenes.

NOTE: If you wish to make the scenes even simpler, you could opt for narrated tableaus.

- **BETWEEN-ACT FILLERS**: Filling in a bit of dead time while one class leaves the stage and another enters is often necessary. In such cases, it is fun to have some little in-front-of-the-curtains diversions. As a rule, these are best performed by older students, but some young, self-confident students are wonderful at these too.

a. Ventriloquist and dummy: One student sits on the other's knee and pretends to be the "dummy" (make-up such as bright red dots on the cheeks helps). Then the ventriloquist and the dummy can tell jokes, discuss school happenings...whatever. Naturally, the ventriloquist will have difficulty with the dummy, who often speaks out of turn. Students can improvise some riotously funny scenes.

b. Commercials: Use well-known TV commercials and change them slightly. For example, a commercial for coffee that will "win your man" enacted by Scarlett O'Hara and Rhett Butler is hilarious. Or, create a commercial for an unknown ridiculous product, such as smart pills. I usually make this task a contest, and the students who come up with the most entertaining commercials will be the ones to demonstrate between acts. Presenting commercials at general assemblies works well too.

c. Did you know?: One or two students simply share with the audience some interesting facts about the school or the teachers. For example, a student might note, "Did you know that there are 121 more boys than girls in this school?" Other interesting facts might include the name of any teacher recently married, or expecting, the name of any student who has recently received acclaim either in or out of school and humorous "in" happenings, such as how much coffee is consumed in the staffroom.

NOTE: Teachers should censor all material for inappropriate content prior to presentation.

d. Bag man performance: Students will do almost anything silly if their heads are disguised by paper bags with small eye holes. Set them loose to sing, dance, tell jokes...whatever.

The key to between-act diversions is to keep them short and saucy and not be overly concerned with skill. Entertain and enjoy!

D. Class Parties

> Murphy's Law: On the day of the class party you'll awaken with a splitting headache!

Parties don't have to be catastrophic, headache-producing nightmares! But good parties don't just happen. Since you can't avoid presenting some, and in many ways, you *do* present them to your students, then plan to prepare them effectively.

You can work with committees if you have older students; however, with younger students, you are entirely responsible for organizing the party. In either case, your creativity, imagination and patience, as well as specific party planning, will make or break the party.

Food and Drinks

You don't seem to be able to have a party without food and drinks, so here are a few guidelines.

- Assign certain people to bring specific items; limit the amount as too much will just end up on the floor.
- Consider choosing a food theme. For example, you could have any of the following:
  a. Health foods: veggies, crackers, cheese
  b. Red foods (valentines): red-iced cookies, apples, red drinks
  c. Mexican foods: tacos, fruits
  d. Chinese foods: fortune cookies, green tea (can just be green drinks), noodles
- Remember that the type of food depends on the age of your students. Younger children love sticky sweet things like cup-

cakes; adolescents (and would-be adolescents in Grade 6) like chips and pop.

- A great idea for Grade 5 students and up is the box social. To avoid boy/girl problems I simply divide the class into two groups, one to make the lunches and one to eat; we exchange roles at the next party. Boxes could be bought for play money or for a bit of real money if your class has a project requiring funds.

- I have found that the best solution to drinks is to have everyone bring what they want, mix the drinks together in a big punch bowl, and add a box of ice cream. Presto! Instant Crazy punch! A piece of dry ice in the bowl makes it an exciting witches' brew for Halloween; a few floating holly sprigs and candy canes hanging around the edge make a Christmas Santa's punch. Food coloring can make the punch any color you want, if it looks "yucky." And as long as you keep an eye on what goes into the punch, it's definitely drinkable.

Decorations

A party is not a party without decorations, so add them to your organization list. If students are old enough, establish a decorating committee. Otherwise, even a few decorations put up by you can make a big difference.

- Easy decorations are balloons. Hang in bunches from curtains or the ceiling or attach one to each desk, perhaps. You could also try long coils of curly ribbons, a large greeting written on the board with colored chalk, and streamers (ever popular, but a bit more trouble to put up).

- Lots of ready-made decorations are available in stores near any special date, but having students make decorations themselves ahead of time is more practical and heightens interest in the party. Since older students like contests, have a best decoration contest, with the prize being something appropriate to the party, for example, a candy cane.

Party Games

All the old, tried-and-true party games are still enjoyable with a few revisions for the classroom.

- **MUSICAL CHAIRS:** If you don't have chairs, mark chalk X's on the floor, or use carpet squares, or even pieces of paper on the floor. To add to the excitement for Junior High students, have them move in pairs so that both partners have to sit on one chair. Hilarious!

- **SCAVENGER HUNTS:** All kinds of items can be located within the classroom with simple cues. For example, ask students to find something long and hollow (straw), something that undoes what you do (eraser), something both round and straight (protractor). Of course, weather permitting, you can send them outside on a real scavenger hunt!

- **SCRAMBLE:** For the old "dive-for-as-many-as-you-can-get" game, use peanuts, poker chips, tokens, anything you can think of. You toss the items around; the person who ends up with the most wins. Or, alternatively, tokens can then be traded in for little prizes: five tokens could buy a candy.

- **UPSET THE ___:** This game is based on Upset the Fruit Basket, but you substitute words appropriate to your party, for example, "Toy-bag" (Christmas), "Pumpkin" (Halloween), "Valentine's Box." One student is "it" and has no place to sit. The student leaves the room while two others change places. The student returns and tries to figure out who has switched. If successful, "it" exchanges places with the first person named. If you want to make this game much more active, "it" can simply call two people's names; they try to switch before "it" takes one of their chairs. Or, "it" can call "switch" and everyone has to switch with someone else, while "it" tries to get a chair! Chaos, but fun!

- **PASS THE ___:** Again an appropriate word is substituted (Pass the valentine/candy cane/pumpkin seed...). Students sit in a circle, hands in fists, arms extended in front of them, fists turned down toward the floor. "It" sits in the middle. One other person (unknown to "it") has the item, which he or she then passes around the circle. All others can pretend to be passing the item. The person who is "it" must locate the item.

- **PIN THE ___:** This version of Pin the Tail on the Donkey is loved even by Junior High students. Depending on the party, the game becomes pin the parts on the haunted house, pin the decorations on the tree, pin the hearts on the Valentine's box, etc. Students are placed in teams of about four or five. Each team lines up about 3 m in front of a large house, tree box, whatever. You can simply outline these images on poster paper (newspaper is too thin). Each team member is given one item (eg., a window or a door) to put on the large picture. Each, in turn, is blindfolded and must walk to and attach his or her part to the picture. The team that gets the most appropriately placed items wins. If older students can do this too easily, turn them around a few times first. An even more hilarious version of this is to make the large picture an outline of a face, and give the team members face parts! Be prepared for some noise!

- **SILENT SEARCH:** In this variation on the familiar guess-who-you-are-from-the-name-on-your-back game, the name of a familiar person, such as Wayne Gretzky, is taped to the back of each student who must discover the identity of the character. Students must get and give information nonverbally. For example, the questioner could mime playing hockey and the answerer could either shake or nod his or her head to indicate whether or not the character played hockey. (Choosing characters with easily actable traits is important, as is modelling a few possible questioning tactics first.) Put a time limit on the game. Many students will not guess their characters' identities, but they should be encouraged to remember what they have learned about the characters and to share the information later.

As you can see, almost any familiar game can be revitalized for your class party, with a minimum of preparation or necessary supplies. Here are a few additional ideas which may be new to you.

- **BALLOON VOLLEY:** Suspend a string across the room, move the desks, and play volleyball with a balloon.
- **HIDDEN (EGGS, HEARTS, CANDY, FRUIT):** Before students enter the room, hide either the real items or little pictures or word symbols of them around the room. Students hunt for them, and keep what they find or trade for the real items.
- **NAME GAME:** You can divide a Junior High class into two groups. All sit on the floor, one group on each side of a blanket. The two people holding the blanket up point to a person on either side. Those two persons stand (still hidden by the blanket). On the count of ''3,'' the blanket is dropped, and each standing person must call out the name of the other standing person. The first one to say the correct name wins, and that person's team receives a point.
- **INDOOR TRACK-MEET RELAYS:** They require more organization,

but work well with students of all ages. You will need the assistance of a couple of aides, parents, or well-trained students to manage one successfully, but the results are rewarding.

Your first task is to place the students in groups. There are different ways of achieving this and letting students have fun at the same time. All of my recommendations call for the random selection, by students, of items from a "hat." Items are as follows: (a) colored pieces of paper, (b) related words on paper (e.g., all flowers), (c) broken compound words to be matched (e.g., "mail" and "carrier," (d) family names (e.g., a team including Grandpa Hartford and Baby Hartford), (e) jelly beans — matching colors, and (f) animal names for which students must make the appropriate sounds to find their groups. Students in like categories form teams — you should plan to create about four teams.

Any minimum-movement relay races or team activities will work, but I found the following the best.

a. Straw javelin: Students hurl straws from behind a line and earn team points depending upon the distance thrown.

b. Cotton ball shot-put: Just what the name implies.

c. Accuracy toss: Cotton balls or paper wads are thrown at a target. Points are earned according to where the balls hit.

d. Balloon carry: Two teams run against each other with the first player batting a balloon with a rhythm stick across the room and back. The second player already has a stick and must take the balloon over without touching it with anything but the stick. Each team needs two sticks and one balloon. (Have extra balloons ready in case of breaks.)

e. Balloon pass: The object is to pass the balloon from one person to another without touching it with hands or arms, then back again to the front of the row. All teams can play at once.

f. Water pass: For this you'll need a teaspoon, a bowl of water, and a graduated cylinder for each group. The bowl of water is at the front of the row; the cylinder is at the back. The object is to transfer the water from the bowl to the cylinder in the spoon. Each person passes the spoon to the person behind. After the last person puts the water (or what's left of it) in the cylinder, that person runs to the front and the passing starts again. Once everyone is back in their original positions, the team with the most water wins. I have found it necessary to put a time limit (5 to 10 min) on this game as some teams will take forever! However, the game is quiet.

g. Balloon shaving: Save this fun, but messy game for last. Each team sits on the newspaper-covered floor and has a balloon blown up tightly, covered with shaving cream, and two small, disposable razors. On signal they must shave the balloon, making sure each person has a turn. If the balloon breaks, they can get another, but will lose valuable time in the process. After a set time (about 3 min), the team with the cleanest balloon wins. (HINT: Be alert for kids rubbing the cream off. Doing so calls for disqualification!)

The key to a good indoor track meet is an empty room (can you put your desks in the hall for the time?) and lots of helpers. Enjoy!

Pacing the Party

A party that gets out of hand due to too many high-action activities together is difficult to retrieve. Consequently, when planning your party, be sure to mix low-key games with more energetic ones. Arrange to have the food break close to the end of the allotted time, immediately after what you expect will be the loudest activity. Also, before the party ever begins, establish a cue (whistle, perhaps?) to which the students must react by freezing; you may need to take control and change activities.

Always be prepared for the possibility that you might run out of planned activities before dismissal time. Have some music, taped stories or even a short film ready to divert those now hyperactive students.

Presenting a fun-for-all party takes a lot of work, but doing it is energy well spent. Since school parties cannot be avoided, plan to present yours with pizzazz! Remember, even if your party doesn't go according to plan, it certainly wouldn't go well, if you hadn't planned. And although your focus is on ensuring that your students enjoy themselves, don't forget to enjoy yourself, too. Be glad when your students show their excitement and joy, and delight in their antics and high spirits!

CHAPTER 6

Organizing

A. Organization and Time Management

> Murphy's Law of Organization: When you finally get
> around to cleaning out your files, you'll throw out
> something you'll need the next day.

The golden rule of teaching is Be prepared, and because being
prepared in the midst of confusion and disorganization is quite
impossible, every teacher must deal with the issue of organization. Organization does not necessarily mean a tidy desk, but it
does mean an awareness of where things are, some degree of consistency in filing, and a knowledge of what is happening when
and what time-line expectations must be met.

Adopting a few basic rules of organization and time management will greatly enhance your teaching as well as help to reduce
or eliminate stress. As you know, there is enough stress in teaching already.

Because time itself is one of the teacher's most valuable com-
modities, any techniques that prevent time loss are important. Perhaps some of the following suggestions will be of benefit to you.

- Laminate a blank seating plan of your class, on heavy card,
  and then use washable flow pens to fill in students' names.
  When seat changes are made, you will not have to redo the
  entire plan. In addition, names can be color-coded for any reason you wish, for example, red for students in Book 1. You
  can even separate girls' and boys' names by color if you have
  a lot of names that don't readily lend themselves to easy sex
  recognition. In this way, a substitute teacher can quickly get
  a grasp of who's who.
- Keep a large wall calendar on which you indicate all upcoming
  events and expectations for the month (e.g., field trips, exams).
  Also invest in a large, secretary-style desk calendar for your-

seating plan (roster)

self, so you can see at a glance what your own expectations are. You can keep both personal and job-related information here, for example, a dental appointment and parent conferences.

- Each month provide students with a photocopy of a calendar page that has room for writing on it. They can fill in important events as well as individual assignments or personal commitments (much like your desk calendar). Even if the calendars end up in the trash right away, students are learning the importance of organization themselves.

- Keep a separate binder for each subject you teach, and place into it all notes, tests, and assignments that you gave to the students. Then you will have a master of the entire subject for students who have been absent or have lost their own copies, for parents who may wish to see what is going on, and, of course, for your own record and test-writing reference. Students may wish to check their own binders occasionally against the master to be sure they are up-to-date. If you find it difficult to keep the master binder complete, delegate the task to a conscientious student whose self-esteem could use a little boost.

- Familiarize yourself with the curriculum guide for whatever you are teaching. Establish goals for both yourself and the students, long and short term! Decide on areas to be covered each month, then break these down into weekly goals. (Daily goals may be unrealistic; often a goal is missed on an assigned day, but picked up on another.) Nothing is hard or impossible if you break it down into small jobs. This form of organization, although time consuming, is mandatory if you are to have any idea of where you are going and what your expectations for your students should be.

- Two or three times yearly, list, in point form, the specifics covered to date in each subject area. Doing so provides you with an account of where you are, as opposed to where you wish to go. Naturally, these records can be shared with students, parents and principal, as all have a vested interest in what is being taught in your class.

- Keep a special binder for students' grades on assignments and tests. The modern computer programs for recording and weighing marks are excellent, but have your binder of marks as well. Not only is it more portable than a computer, but it provides you with an accurate backup copy. Keep your grade records up-to-date! Color-coding each subject may be of assistance.

NOTE: Color-coding different classes really helps when you teach the same subject several times a day. Marks causing concern can be circled for quick identification and further reference.

Sometimes, reliable students can be trained to enter marks for you, saving you time. If there is a concern about confidentiality of marks, then do not allow students to record those marks. However, as every teacher knows, there are many marks, such as group marks for an oral presentation where all marks are common knowledge anyway, that can be student-recorded. When students act as teacher aides, their self-esteem is boosted. Most really love to help out, and you should expect to provide tokens of thanks, as well.

- Allow yourself a special time each day, either before or after school, depending on when you are most productive, for planning and preparation. Time management specialists encourage using the same time period daily, as our brains will then develop a readiness to plan at this time. Even the most seasoned teachers need to plan and to check their progress against curriculum and individual needs.

- Once a year, discard old masters and reorganize your files. Doing so is much like sorting through your closet and getting rid of clothes you never wear! An overabundance of collected materials often means that none will be used; there are too many from which to choose. Keep only your best materials and constantly upgrade and update these. Don't allow yourself to become a paper packrat!

- If keeping your desk tidy is a problem for you, train a few dependable students to do it for you — they really love this responsibility! As long as the students know a few basics, such as what not to discard and where you like certain items, they can keep your desk looking good very efficiently. Reward them in some small way, such as taking them to McDonald's periodically, for their time and effort.

- Keep a special file or box near your desk and in it place all memos and junk mail you get in your mailbox. Then clean out the file when you have time within the next month. Otherwise, as Murphy's Law warns, if you get into the habit of emptying your mailbox into the nearest garbage can, you are certain to discard something important.

- Use the stacking plastic storage bins available everywhere for keeping things like journals, free-time activity sheets, spelling books, workbooks, and class coloring materials. At Junior High these bins are great for individual time sheets, homework sheets, etc. Have specific Hand In boxes — color-coded for different subjects or classes. Inform students early in the year that you will be responsible only for work that has been placed in the Hand In box. Not accepting work put on your desk or handed to you as you leave the school, for example, eliminates the problem of students insisting work has been handed in when you cannot find it!

- Get into the habit of making lists. List things to be done daily and check them off as you accomplish them. Keep a pad of paper in a special spot at home (beside the bed works well for me) and immediately jot down ideas as they pop into your head (at 3 a.m. no doubt!) A certain sense of accomplishment comes with completing all the items on your Today list. Keeping lists is an integral component of time management.

- Keep a special file for parents' correspondence. Avoid the temptation to discard even brief notes. File all the notes away in one place. Chances are you'll need them later.

- As far as students' desks and lockers are concerned, at least some will be messy no matter what you do, and how they organize their space is really up to them. However, you can provide a specific brief time each week for desk or locker cleaning. If at all possible, make this cleaning time the same time each week. The consistency will help to train the students to be more organized. As a rule, keep textbooks out of desks and stacked neatly in the room to create more individual desk space. Try to provide younger students with cubby holes or individual stackable plastic baskets. If your students are reasonably organized, you will waste less time helping them find materials or providing new copies, and they will not constantly experience the frustration of lost items.

- Tape a small class schedule to the corner of your desk or to the pull-out ledge if your desk has one. You can always see at a glance where you and the students should be. You can promote a similar awareness in Junior High students by providing several such timetables for binders, home, pockets, lockers,

101

etc. Chances are they will still check your copy regularly!

- Keep a running list on your desk of needed supplies or items. Carry the list with you when you shop. Nothing is more frustrating than forgetting that one small item for the science experiment when you were right beside it at the store.

- Keep paper and pencil in your car, at your bedside, on your fridge — any place where you spend a lot of time — because good ideas will often pop into your head at the most inopportune moments, and if not instantly recorded, may well be lost forever. If your brilliant ideas make themselves known to you during the night, don't fret. Get up, write down your thoughts, and return to bed.

- Keep stacks of worksheets and photocopied pages neat and accessible. Here are a few of many ways to do so.
  a. Stand soap or cereal boxes, painted in art, on their sides. Cover with plasticized shelf paper for greater durability.
  b. Use coffee tins, decorated in art, for completed papers waiting to go home. You can curl the papers slightly to fit into the tins.
  c. Get cardboard shoe racks from stores such as Canadian Tire or Ikea.
  d. Turn to building supply stores or stationery stores for collating shelves or stacking bins.

Above all, don't waste time worrying about all the many things you, as a teacher, are expected to accomplish. You may *never* be caught up; new responsibilities so quickly replace old. Categorize your duties and tackle them systematically. Remember that you can do only what you can do! Don't take on more than you can handle, but if you do, don't be afraid to delegate duties or ask for help.

Believe in yourself. If you conscientiously give yourself a little time and make a bit of effort, you *can* organize the cloud of confusion that hangs over you.

B. Monthly Review Checklist

In addition to payday, the end of the month signifies the time to fulfill responsibilities such as completing reports, attending staff meetings and updating records. I have also found that to further organization and self-evaluation, I should perform some other duties which I have outlined on a monthly checklist that I have created and to which I refer toward the end of each month. Depending on the grade you teach, as well as your own personality, your checklist will vary from mine, but the basic ideas will remain the same. Here is a summary of work you may want to ensure that you do monthly. The basic checklist that appears on page 104 reflects this summary.

a. Review goals and objectives to see which have been mastered and which need to be renewed.
b. Establish goals and objectives for the following month, based on ''a.''
c. Send home to parents a simple form which notes any assignments late or undone, any problems and a positive point or two. (Trust the mail more than hand delivery.) You thus keep parents up-to-date on their children's work.
d. Make a point of calling two or three parents with whom you've had no contact this month.
e. Order films, kits, or other supplies for the next month, based on your goals and objectives. Purchase immediately the art or science supplies you will need for the month.
f. Make a quick list of copying, typing, laminating and other services that you know you will need for the upcoming month. In this way, if you have the services of an aide or student helper, you will know exactly what they can do to help.
g. Prepare your new Theme Board (if you are teaching thematically) and change any displays that have been up for the past month.
h. Fill in and display a new calendar sheet with all the upcoming events.
i. Check with the librarian to see what students have books overdue (your concern will be appreciated) and make a point of following up with the students involved.
j. Visit a store catering to teachers to rekindle your enthusiasm and borrow novel ideas. I always limit myself to a small amount of money and leave my VISA card at home.
k. Replenish your classroom supplies of glue, scissors, pens, and so on so that you are not constantly running to the office or store room. Short trips for supplies are time wasters!
l. Clean the room and desks (with students' help, of course).

MONTHLY REVIEW CHECKLIST

GOALS/OBJECTIVES	Achieved	Not Yet Achieved
_____	_____	_____
_____	_____	_____
_____	_____	_____

NEW GOALS/OBJECTIVES

_____

_____

_____

LETTER SENT HOME   yes ☐ no ☐

PARENTS CALLED: _____

_____

_____

ORDERS TO BE MADE: _____

_____

HELP NEEDED: _____

_____

THEME BOARD yes ☐ no ☐   CALENDAR yes ☐ no ☐

LIBRARIAN: Books overdue _____

_____

CLASSROOM SUPPLIES NEEDED: _____

_____

You may not earn any kudos for being organized and accountable, but by being so, you have, at least in part, earned your paycheque. So, cash your cheque and allow yourself a little splurge! You deserve it! You are — after all — *a teacher*!

C. Time-out for Sanity

Despite all your tasks and responsibilities — or maybe because of them — I would like to urge you to take time, that resource you need to manage so efficiently, to renew and refresh your spirits.

Every teacher needs to, because every teacher knows the distressing sensation of being stretched like an elastic band to the point of snapping. Frequently, this tension accompanies us home, perhaps to ruin an otherwise pleasant evening, and sometimes even casting a pall over the next morning.

But you can turn to some quick pick-me-ups that allow mini-escapes from anxiety, and with these, a chance to re-energize.

I have developed several Anxiety-Attack Antidotes (AAA) and have practised these frequently both during the day (if I can steal a few moments) and at the end of a particularly bad day, with varying degrees of success. Most take only 10 min. Perhaps some of these self-preservation techniques will be valuable to you. At the very least they may give you a starting point from which you can create your very own antidotes to take on time-outs.

- **PEACEFUL POETRY:** Capitalize on the calming effect of poetry by reading a few poems by a favorite poet. (I like Rod McKuen and Shelley.) Choose books with the type of poems you personally enjoy, and revel in the special sensation that comes from sitting in a quiet space reading poems. A file of poems collected from magazines, journals, even students' work, is great. Be sure to save these special poems just for anxiety-attack antidote occasions.
- **HILARIOUS HUMOR:** Take 10 min to enjoy something funny. Good choices are books of education-related jokes or just about any of the vast number of books available in the humor section of bookstores. One of my favorites, which never fails to provoke a smile, is *Revolting Rhymes* by Roald Dahl. Reading this type of material after a particularly trying day can give you a whole new perspective on teaching, and indeed, on life itself.
- **SOULFUL SONGS:** Make, or buy, a tape of your favorite mellow songs — I particularly like "The Rose" sung by Bette Midler and "A Return to Romance" by Zamfir. When you need a time-out, turn off the lights in your classroom, lock the door, and enjoy the music. Force yourself to concentrate on the lyrics and the flow of the melodies, and not on the disastrous day you've just endured. As soon as a negative thought pops into your head (and they will!), say "no" out loud, and force your mind back to the music. This type of meditation allows both mind and body to relax. If your classroom is unavailable or

not relaxing, try the nurse's room, a corner of the library, or even a storage room.

- **GOOD NEWS NOTES:** Keep a journal (I make entries daily regardless of my anxiety level) in which you can jot down at least one positive thing that happened on an otherwise difficult day. There will be times when you are convinced that absolutely nothing positive occurred, but you will always come up with something if you think about the day honestly. Recording the event, no matter how small, affirms it in the mind and brings a little rush of relief in the knowledge that the day was not all bad. Reading back through previously written journal pages can be uplifting too.

- **CARING CALL:** Select a parent with whom you haven't had much communication, and phone with some positive information about his/her child. The piece of information doesn't have to be about an academic achievement. Perhaps Ryan shared his crayons without being asked to. Maybe Cara completed all her homework. Perhaps Mark volunteered an interesting concept during a discussion. You could even note something as simple as the scoring of a goal in floor hockey. Sharing something good with a parent will make you both feel better!

- **WISE WORDS:** Listening, even for a few minutes, to the words of a good speaker discussing any relevant topic such as stress management or relaxation techniques can work wonders. My favorite is Barbara Coloroso's tape *Discipline: Kids Are Worth It.* Coloroso is so practical and down to earth that her words of wisdom always remind me that I am not feeling frustrated alone. Good tapes on many topics are readily available.

- **LONELY LETTER:** Psychologists have long acknowledged that putting thoughts on paper promotes inner cleansing. So, write to yourself, accurately describing some of the day's most difficult moments. Don't hesitate to make your language as colorful as you want to (no one is going to read it but you!), but if you get too carried away, you may want to destroy your letter immediately after reading it. Sometimes reading the letter over when you are finished will make you laugh at the ludicrous things that happened, and, of course, laughter is therapeutic!

- **WINNING WALK:** Quickly, without stopping to talk to anyone, walk around the outside of the school yard once or even twice, time permitting. The faster the walk the better. You can even run if you feel up to it and are wearing sensible shoes. Fitness fanatics will attest to the value of exercise in relieving anxiety, so, no matter how exhausted you feel, try taking a short, winning walk. Focus only on how your body feels during the walk. Listen to the beat of your heart, your breathing, then come back to your room feeling refreshed.

- **OVERWORKED OTHERS:** A sure-fire way to forget your own problems is to focus on helping someone else who is in need. In any school there is always someone — perhaps the secretary, the custodian, the librarian, or another teacher — who would be glad of 10 min of your time. A colleague once came to me after school and said, "I have 10 min. What can I do for you?" I was shocked, then pleased, by her offer. I was in the middle of trying to record marks in several places at once, and her help was greatly appreciated. Unexpected and unconditional, it was, I am sure, a pick-me-up for both of us.

- **SOMETHING SPECIAL:** Keep on hand, in a special AAA drawer, a small selection of favorite teas, coffees or snacks. (I try to keep a few precious, individually wrapped Belgian chocolates on hand.) When your anxiety level threatens to reach the danger zone, sweeten the situation with a special treat.

You can, of course, easily combine this antidote with one of the other antidotes for a potent effect! (Imagine drinking creamy mocha and listening to sounds of the sea.) Just avoid the temptation to use special goodies unless they are really warranted.

Plan to use any or all of these little pick-me-ups as often as necessary. If you are suffering greatly from stress, you can't afford not to. Take the time to be good to yourself. You are not pampering yourself; you are seeking to preserve your sanity! And you may enjoy unexpected benefits. Once, after a particularly harrowing morning, I opened my AAA drawer as my students were exiting for lunch. One perceptive youngster exclaimed with genuine concern, "Oh, oh! She's opening her AAA drawer! We'd better be good this afternoon."

And they were!

CHAPTER 7

Coping

Mistakes are simply invitations to try again.
— *Dian Ritter*

If we believe this quotation, then many teachers are trying again with those very special students who are now being parachuted into "normal" classrooms. Although the psychology behind the integration may be wonderful, so many problems are presented by these students — problems to which we have yet to find practical solutions — that the average teacher, with a class of about 25 "normal" students (what is "normal" anyway?) and two or three "special" students is overwhelmed.

I have taught such a class — not very successfully I might add. But I have learned a few techniques that may be of some use to other teachers in the same situation. Many of the ideas suggested under "Determining Logical (and Palatable) Consequences" (pages 39-48) may be helpful; rather than be redundant, I will identify types of problem students and suggest a few techniques for dealing with each. Since *Help!* is not a book of whys but of hows, possible reasons for any of the problems discussed will not be given. Teachers will take these into consideration before trying any types of intervention. And remember that, although I have categorized interventions, any of the techniques can be used effectively with different types of special students.

A. The Hyperactive Student

First, let us agree that "hyperactive student" tends to be a catch-all label for every student who acts up and doesn't follow the rules without a fight. We all know who the hyperactive students are after the first day of school. Some of them may already be tagged with "Behavior Problem" labels. Great! So how do we deal with them in our regular classrooms?

- First, establish a rapport with such students, and try to win them over to your side. You must be sincere to do this. If you succeed, you might be able to reason with the student about his or her behavior. Of course, reasoning only works if the child can control the hyperactivity. Usually the child can't!
- Don't even try to restrain him (it's usually a "him") to his desk. Allow him to work wherever he will settle, be it on the window ledge, under a desk or table, even at your desk (make sure he realizes that being able to do this is a privilege). Just get him to work — no matter where!
- Allow the student frequent breaks. Send him or her on little errands; allow bathroom breaks even when you know they are unnecessary; ask the student to deliver messages — anything to permit legitimate movement.
- Be sure to give lavish praise for those times when the student *is* sitting somewhere working and not interfering with others. Too often we see these times as little reprieves, breathe a sigh of relief, and forget to acknowledge them to the child.
- Seat this child at the back rather than at the front of the class. Although this advice goes against all the old wisdom about having the problem child close to you and at the front of the room, consider this. When seated at the front, every time the child gets up, fights, or acts up in some way, the entire class is an audience; they all have a perfect view of his or her antics. If the child is in a back, corner seat, the only students affected are those few nearby.
- Use this student in some leadership capacity where he or she is responsible for the behavior of others. A little responsibility can be calming. For example, you might ask the student to keep the daily attendance. (You also benefit if a student can take over this job well.)
- If necessary, use a contract system, where you and the student establish a list of inappropriate behaviors, then select one or two behaviors on which to concentrate. Draw up a contract indicating the allowable frequency of each behavior and what the consequences will be for improvement, lack of improvement, etc. This techniques works with some students — usually older ones, but they have to be really excited about the consequences.

- Isolate the student as a last resort, but never do this as a surprise. Establish a quiet place for isolation: often another teacher will be willing to have an isolation desk for your students if you have one for that teacher's students in your classroom. (Cardboard dividers or carrels turned to the corners work well.) Discuss with the student the possible reasons for asking him or her to go to the isolation place. Point out that he or she will get a lot more done and not be distracted by others. Eventually, many students will ask to go to the isolation desk so that they can work.

Remember that you are not going to change the hyperactive student into a quiet little mouse. And thank goodness for that. Where would our world be without hyperactive workaholics who tend to be the instigators and creators? Accept hyperactive students as they are, and try to work within the boundaries of their energy levels.

B. The Angry Student

The angry student gives way to temper tantrums or fights frequently.

- Be alert to mood swings in this type of child. There is usually some sort of clue that a fight or tantrum is on the way. Step in at this point and create a distraction. For example, you might send the child on an errand or solicit the child's help in some way.
- If a student *has* lost control and is storming out, the age of the student determines how you react. A younger child cannot be allowed to leave in anger lest he or she comes to some harm. An older child (10+) should be allowed to go. Give the child some time to cool down. Don't impede the exit, but say (or shout if need be), "I'll be waiting for you. We'll talk when you get back." In this way you are allowing the student to keep his or her dignity and letting the student know that you care enough to want to discuss matters at a convenient time. Just be sure to follow through and seek the student out later.
- If two students are fighting, whether or not to intervene is entirely your own decision. I have always sought to stop the fight, if for no other reason than I can't bear to watch children get hurt; I have suffered a black eye and a fat lip on two

separate occasions for this weakness. However, if you *do* decide to intervene, first send another student for help, shout loudly at the fighters, and try to separate them. Usually other students will come to your assistance, or the fighters will stop in order to avoid hitting you. Once both have cooled down, you will want to take further measures: play down rather than build up a fight, so as to give it minimum reinforcement.

- You may, unfortunately, be confronted by violence in the classroom, especially at the higher grade levels. If, for example, an angry student suddenly pulls a knife out and begins to threaten you or your students with it, assume that the student is out of control. Quietly ask all the other students to leave, and ask a specific student to go to the office for assistance. Keep your voice calm. Do not try to approach the angry student or to take the knife away. Maintain eye contact with the student if possible. Stay with him or her, but maintain a safe distance. Talk calmly until help comes. The only time you might decide to take physical action is if another student is being endangered — how to react in a violent incident depends a lot on your personal makeup and physical abilities.

- If a student has a temper tantrum, have spectators move aside to ensure their safety. If you are bigger and stronger than the student (not usually the case at Junior High), you may wish to restrain him — the offender is probably a boy — by crossing his arms in front of him, and holding him securely from behind. If doing this is impossible, then stay with the student, removing dangerous objects when possible, until he cools down. Stay calm, but don't patronize the student. Avoid pat psychology phrases such as "I know how you feel...." You have no idea how that student is feeling then. Later, when he is calm, you can discuss the situation honestly. For instance, instead of saying, "You must have been under a lot of stress," say "Boy, were you ever mad!" The student will relate much better to an open, honest evaluation of what happened. "You know I've felt like killing someone sometimes when I've been really mad like that. Want to go for a walk and talk about it?" If he says "no," leave it at that. If he goes with you, you've passed the first test!

Don't dwell on the first occurrence of any angry outburst. However, if outbursts continue, then establish some guidelines with the student. Decide what you can do together to prevent further incidents. Ask how you can help. Try to find out what precipitates the tantrums and prevent these situations if possible. Work with the student, rather than against.

C. The Slow Student

Having students who just can't keep up is a very common problem. Usually these students, both "special" integrated ones and "normal" ones, are not behavior problems. They are, however, often frustrated by their own inabilities. Often they are not reading at anywhere near the level expected for the class in which they have been placed. Here are a few strategies for helping them.

- Peer tutoring is wonderful. Having same-age peers or students from an older class come and work with the student(s) at a specific time each day is great for both the student and the tutor.
- Teacher tutoring is important too. Establish a time when you will be available for individual assistance (eg., 8 to 8:45 a.m. on Wednesday) and *be there*. Then it is up to the students to come to you. Once they realize you are serious and that you will always be there, they'll come.
- Incorporate a catch-up class or two into your weekly agenda. Slower students can get caught up, while students who are on top of everything are given choices such as free reading, crosswords, peer tutoring and word searches. Keep a file of such activities up-to-date at all times.
- Always help the slow student to get started. As soon as you have given the entire class directions, go directly to the slow student, and start him or her off. Help the student write the first sentence or do the first problem. Ask the student what he or she will do next, and leave only when the student can give you a specific answer.
- Arrange for exams to be read to such students (unless you are testing reading). In core subjects such as Science and Social Studies, failing a slow reader simply because he or she only got half-way through the test is unfair.
- Allow slow students to use all the mechanical devices available to you. Tomorrow's citizens will not have to do long division or metric conversions in their heads. Let's be realistic. Give the students calculators, keyboards, computers, and audio tapes

112

(with audio directions instead of written directions).

- Find a type of pen/pencil and writing paper that the student especially likes. Often a fine-tip flow pen is easier to use than a ballpoint pen or a pencil. Experiment with thicknesses of writing tools and with different colors of paper. Try anything!

D. The Withdrawn Student

Let me begin by cautioning you to be aware of the circumstances that appear to be causing the withdrawal of a student, because these will affect your interventions. You will have to do some investigating and serious observing before you take action. I have therefore separated the interventions by possible withdrawal causes.

PHYSIOLOGICAL CAUSES: Sometimes what appears to be withdrawal is actually a reaction to illness, fatigue, general malaise, headache, or the inability to see or hear clearly. Check for these problems before searching for anything more serious.

- Intervention: Check with a parent to see whether the parent feels the child may be physically ill; express your concerns and suggest the child be taken to a medical doctor. If the parent seems unco-operative, inform the school nurse of the situation.

A MANIPULATIVE TOOL: Amazing as it may seem, some children have mastered the skill of conscious withdrawal and use it to control their environment. With a limited expenditure of energy, the child may be receiving constant encouragement, support, and persuasion from care givers hoping for a response.

- Intervention: Ignoring the child when he or she is obviously withdrawing and reinforcing any opposite behaviors is the best way to deal with this awkward situation. You may also need to intercept overly helpful peers in their zealous attempts to assist you.

FEAR AND INSECURITY: This type of withdrawal is the most common and, unfortunately, the most difficult to treat. In this case, the child is too afraid to do anything — speak, act, react, or interact — lest failure and its consequences result. The reasons for this fear may be deep-seated and varied. It is not the teacher's role to attempt to treat the underlying causes, but rather to recognize the child's fear and deal with it appropriately.

- Interventions:
  a. Provide low-key, one-to-one assistance in areas of difficulty, and set up situations for success by breaking work into small components, then providing rewards, social or otherwise, for completion of these assignments.
  b. Ask the child to assist you with small tasks at recesses, noons, etc. In this way, you can build rapport, trust and confidence.
  c. Look for an interest or skill the child possesses and pursue it in some way. (For example, if the child plays guitar, plan a specific lesson based on guitars.)
  d. Provide in-class activities for partners, but do not allow students to choose partners, as the withdrawn child will always end up alone. Instead, indicate that you have chosen partners for students randomly; in fact, pair the withdrawn child with another who is compassionate and helpful.
  e. Establish buddies with another class. You can take an older student into your confidence (eg., "Billy is very shy and needs you to act like a big brother. I know you can handle that.") Or a younger buddy (provided that the child is not hyperactive or overconfident) can provide the withdrawn child with a relatively non-threatening chance to be in the helper role.
  f. Turn to the confidence-building activities suggested in Chapter 2 for possible help (see pages 23-32).

A SYMPTOM OF DEPRESSION: Withdrawal due to depression is serious. Childhood psychosis that manifests itself in the form of depression and withdrawal from the world requires the assistance of professionals other than teachers.
- Intervention: You can attempt the interventions mentioned previously, but do *not* try to play psychiatrist. Get help!

There are a few Don'ts to keep in mind when dealing with the withdrawn child, and, in fact, with any child.

1. Don't call on the child to answer when you know the child's thoughts are far away. All you would do is cause embarrassment. Rather, move quickly to the child as you continue teaching, touch him or her lightly to attract attention, and continue.
2. Don't cross-examine or try to force the child to tell you what is wrong. If the child knew, or wanted you to know, he or

she would tell you. Instead, let the child know you are concerned and willing to listen, and leave it at that.

3. Don't force children to socialize. Some individuals prefer to be loners. These children may be using withdrawal as a coping mechanism. Its complete removal may leave them defenceless and vulnerable. Try to respect their right to be alone, at least most of the time.
4. Don't forget the withdrawn child. Doing so is easy, because this child never causes trouble and doesn't interfere with the others. Busy teachers can easily overlook such a child for days at a time.

Although teachers may at times view the withdrawn child as a quiet blessing in the class, they usually worry more about such a child than all the other students combined. However, if any interventions work, watching a withdrawn child finally becoming involved can be very rewarding. Don't give up!

E. The Irresponsible Student

This child causes the teacher's hair to turn grey! You know the student is smart and can do the work, but he or she simply won't! Homework is never done; class work is never completed and not handed in if it is; notes and books seldom arrive with the student to class...the list goes on. The irresponsible student, not necessarily unpleasant or impolite, is characterized by a "who cares?" attitude that drives teachers crazy! What can we do?

- Be sure that the student does, in fact, understand the work. Often what appears to be laziness is an inability to do the work; rather than fail, the student chooses not to try at all. If you suspect this is the case, arrange for a little one-to-one tutoring, make sure that a good mark is earned as a result, and see if this success brings about any difference in attitude.
- Let the student choose how to handle an assignment. For example, if you want a demonstration of the effect of pollution on the environment, give the following choices: (a) poster; (b) essay/report; (c) mobile; (d) collage of collected materials; (e) audio tape of interview.

  Choices can be given in most subject areas. Evaluation becomes more difficult, but by giving choices, you just might hit upon one that sparks the problem child's interest so much that genuine positive reinforcement is earned. And we all know the benefits of that!

- Do *not* take away any thing or activity that is important to the student in an attempt to get the student to work. In other words, avoid the common practice of taking a student out of Physical Education or off a team because of unfinished math, for example. That sport may be the only positive thing in the child's life; take it away, and what is left? Instead, try to exploit the child's interest in this one area. In Language Arts, for example, ask such a student to write about the team or activity. In math, create problems around team scores. And by all means, *watch* this student doing the one thing he or she does well, and compliment the student about it sincerely. Establishing rapport is important, and showing interest in the student is one way to do it.

- Share with this student (and any student for that matter) positive comments made by other teachers. In fact, make up a few if you have to. I once had a student who refused to work for anyone at all. One day I casually mentioned that Mr. Jackson, the Language Arts teacher, really liked him and thought he was trying hard to get his work done. Mr. Jackson had said nothing of the sort, but my strategy worked. The boy in question looked amazed, but came to me the next day to get help with the story I knew he was supposed to be writing. Mr. Jackson (bless his heart) awarded the boy an exceptionally good mark — he was probably totally amazed that anything had been turned in! — and the process had begun. Tell students they are appreciated, and then appreciate them. Believe in them. Imagine an individual's potential as if it were already realized, and your words of encouragement will then be sincere.

- If necessary, a parent can be contacted. Together with the student, express your concerns, and offer some viable suggestions such as the following:
  a. Establish a specific time each night for homework. If none is brought home (a common parental complaint) then the student is to read, write a letter...whatever...for the predesignated length of time. A half-hour is usually enough.
  b. The place where homework is to be done must be as consistent as the time. For example, the student must work from 6:30 to 7 p.m. at the kitchen table, with no phone calls allowed during that time. The reason for the consistency

is that eventually the brain will become accustomed to having to work then, and homework will be a less troublesome task.

c. It may be necessary to start a homework and daily work book that is signed by both parents and teachers daily. I know keeping such a book is bothersome, but sometimes it is the only solution. Often the students hate it so much they eventually learn to manage without it.

d. Sometimes contracts made together with the students and parents are helpful. In some American high schools, parents are paying their children cash to attend classes and work. And I'm not so sure such a motivation is wrong. The older the students get, the more we seem to require extrinsic motivations. Maybe you need to hold out a few carrots. Who says Junior High students can't be bribed with candy? Ideally, the parents and students together would work out a contract, but in reality, the teacher often needs to intervene.

[handwritten margin note: ? I don't think I agree here..]

- Mail home a monthly form letter listing all major assignments done/undone, with a word or two of both encouragement and concern. I don't suggest you do this with every student — there simply aren't enough hours in the day — but identify a few who might benefit.

When dealing with seemingly irresponsible, lazy students, keep in mind that you can't force them to work. Threats and detentions, for the most part, are a waste of time. They merely serve to further alienate the student and increase the teacher's blood pressure. Also, remember that students do mature, and eventually they will want to learn and will work. Until then, perhaps the best you can do is to keep such students in school and off the streets. And never forget that important issue of respect. Don't treat students as if they are stupid (even if that is the impression they give). If you do, they will behave accordingly.

F. The Unruly Class

Every teacher has had one! That curious combination of personalities that, when together in a classroom, are impossible! Alone, each student couldn't be sweeter; together, they make Hell's Angels look like innocents! For whatever reason, certain groupings become teachers' nightmares. Unfortunately, the best solution is to try to protect your sanity until the end of the year, but in the meantime, there are a few ideas that may help you to cope with your difficult class.

- Establish no more than three specific rules and stick to them. Be consistent in your consequences for broken rules.
- Be consistent but not predictable. Constantly shock or amaze your class in any way possible. Present an entire lesson in sign language; bring in a rock video; have a surprise juice break; go for a jog around the school before class. Keep your students guessing!
- Change your seating arrangement regularly so that groups don't have a chance to form. Try irregular seating formations such as semi-circles or squares.
- Establish a signal (e.g., a whistle) for attention, and insist that students respond to it appropriately always.
- Make your worst offenders the leaders. Give them the responsibility of keeping their groups on task. Have groups compete for prizes or points which can be accumulated for later rewards such as extra gym time, earlier dismissal, and cupcakes in class. Never take away points; just award them to a group that is on task when another is not.
- Tell them what you like about them. This type of class very quickly comes to see itself as the ''worst class in the school.'' Once students have established this, they will work very hard to keep up the class image. If you can convince them that they have many admirable qualities, such as their innovativeness, and then solicit their assistance to change their image — make it a group challenge — you just might succeed in eliminating key problems. I once challenged a horrible class to change specific group dynamics, such as out-of-seat behaviors and specific students talking when they weren't supposed to. We appointed a ''secretary'' who kept an accurate account of happenings in other classes as well as in mine. The results were astounding.
- Maintain a positive outlook. Change your own point of view: this class is not a disaster, it is a challenge! Set small goals for yourself, and allow yourself lots of time-outs. (See ''Time-out for Sanity,'' pages 104-107.)

G. The Problem Parent

Most parents are supportive of you, the teacher; but a few, unfortunately, fall into the category of problem parent. Nonetheless, keep in mind that parenting is the most difficult job in the world and that parents are not to blame for all the problems we may see in their children. In most cases, parents are doing the best they can. With this in mind, review the following suggestions for helping you deal with those who seem to require more of your time than others.

- **THE HOMEWORK PARENT:** This is the parent whom you are quite sure is regularly doing John's homework for him. There is little you can do other than giving John the same work to do *in class* and making an objective comparison. Then at the next parent/teacher interview, you can point out the differences in the quality of the work, and ask for the parent's advice.
- **THE OVERPROTECTIVE PARENT:** Try to avoid making an enemy of this parent, as it is easily done! Realize that what the child says is taken as Gospel. Solicit help from the child's parent from a positive point of view. "Carol is doing well. She could do even better if..." "Kyle has a great sense of humor and loves to entertain the class instead of doing his work. Can you help me to show him that his work is important too?" Try to call these parents before they call you, and always lead up to a problem with good news. Remember to compliment some specific thing the parent has done. For example, you might say, "You have done a great job of teaching Jimmy to be polite." Then state your case. Remember, alienating this parent will make your job much tougher and will make the parent even more overprotective of the child.
- **THE INVISIBLE PARENT:** Don't assume that this parent is invisible due to lack of caring: reasons for not being seen include work load, exhaustion, fear, and embarrassment. So make the first move and call the parent with good news only. Send little notes home often, letting the parent know what is happening. Then, if you *do* need to discuss a problem, there is a better chance of the parent showing up.
- **THE ANGRY PARENT:** Parents of this type make themselves known to you early in the year. They are the ones who say they have "had it" with the inefficient school system or whatever. Be very careful here. Remain professional and ethical.

Listen carefully to their complaints, and check out their perceptions of their child carefully. If the parent acts angry in your presence, how will he or she act toward a child about whom a teacher has complained? Will the child receive unfair punishment at home for lack of effort at school? If you even suspect this, try a different tactic. Angry parents are unhappy people. The best you can hope to do is to listen well and not provoke further anger that can harm the child.

- **THE DEFEATED PARENT:** We have all met these. They are the parents who sink into their chairs and look defeated before you say a word. Usually they have heard so many negative comments about their child already that nothing you can say will be news. They have probably tried everything in their power to change the child, but have been unsuccessful, and really are defeated. They are easy to recognize, and when you do, change your tactics immediately. Rather than registering a complaint about the child, or listing off all the things the child does wrong, try a little empathy. Tell them you know they must be having a hard time with _____ as he or she is certainly difficult. Find something positive to share about the child. Then, if you must, bring up no more than one problem area, and be sure to suggest a way that both you and the parents can attack it. *Never* give the impression that you have given up on a child!

H. Checklist of Teacher Behavior

No discussion of problem students and parents would be complete without a review of our own behavior.

You can use a checklist such as the one that follows to remind yourself of how you should be dealing with your students, their parents and your peers. Answer each question honestly, and quiz yourself about once a month. If you have more than five negative answers, there is a problem worth investigating.

CHECKLIST OF TEACHER BEHAVIOR

DO I...

1. Remember that I am dealing with children, not adults, and treat them accordingly?
2. Avoid judging one child by the actions of another?
3. Always try to be honest and trustworthy in my dealings with the students?
4. Avoid showing prejudice or obviously choosing favorites among students?
5. Respect the parents and their efforts with their children?
6. Come to class well prepared, at least most of the time?
7. Praise peers' relations with students rather than being jealous or suspicious of them?
8. Willingly admit when I am wrong?
9. Appreciate the many assets of my position as teacher?
10. Practise the principle of *never* giving up on a child?

CHAPTER 8

Enjoying

*I will...because I **can**!*

Teaching today is probably more difficult and much less rewarding than ever before. Certainly, students seem to be less motivated, less capable, less energetic and more apathetic every year. And teachers, although probably trained better than their predecessors, are shaking their heads in dismay; too often they are overwhelmed by a feeling of "why bother?" This is the question that this final chapter addresses. Although I do not profess to have found a cure or even a bandage for the problems confronting teachers today, I have a few ideas that should help any teacher whose hope is faltering.

A. Why Teach?

Never before have individuals needed education more than in the highly technical, yet struggling world of today. On one hand, the human race is taking giant strides in the sciences and technological fields; on the other, disasters surround us. Now is not a time for teachers to lose sight of their goal, the preparation of the young to run the world of tomorrow, amid the horrors of wars, disease, famine, pollution, and crime. Preparing the young is a lofty goal, and one that only teachers can truly address! This is why, as teachers in a society that offers us limited recognition, we push ourselves to educate children, even those who don't seem to want our help.

There are, as I see it, three specific reasons to compel us to teach.

1. If we don't educate for the future, *then who will?* Parents are already pushed to extremes with the raising of their children and need the full support of educators. We must work as partners, whenever possible, to prepare the young.

2. Children, despite all their efforts to imperil our survival, are worth it!
3. We have chosen our profession freely; we should make the most of it.

Let us keep in mind the importance of our roles as teachers, as well as ways to keep our spirits up.

- Remember that teachers *do* make a great impact on their students.
- Be glad you have a job that is relatively secure.
- Feel privileged that you work with young people. No matter how difficult and unreachable they seem to be, they still harbor within them a wonderful energy and idealism. You have a chance to benefit from that.
- Remember that you *do* have two months off every summer to renew yourself (yes, I know it's necessary — but what if you *didn't* get it?), as well as Christmas and spring holidays.
- Accept the fact that sometimes it's OK to just babysit or rely on busywork.
- You *are* human and have limitations. Learn to delegate responsibilities. Don't take on more than you can comfortably handle; ask for help if you need it.
- Learn what little pickups work best for you (see ''Time-out for Sanity'' in Chapter 6), and use them.
- Take a rest and recreation (R and R) day and visit flea markets, magic and joke stores, hobby stores, magazine and bookstores, toy stores and teachers' stores. You don't have to buy anything — just look for new ideas to borrow.
- Do your best to lighten up your approach to teaching. Try to see the humor in the classroom and enjoy some of your students' antics.
- Remember that intermittent reinforcement, the reinforcement of appropriate behaviors at unpredictable times, still works! Use it!
- Do something amusing, original or totally bizarre one day — wear your old, battered hat to try to shock those apathetic kids!
- If things really seem to be going downhill, stop, re-evaluate, and change your expectations of yourself, your students, or both. Don't be overcritical of yourself. You can always try again tomorrow!
- Don't be afraid to take a break on a bad day. Show a movie,

have a "cake break," or just go outside for a walk with your class. Curriculum and time lines are not rigid. Be flexible.

- Use as many aids as possible: peer teaching; videos; audio cassettes; project teaching; school exchange of students/teachers for specific days' subjects/activities; guests such as doctors, police, and zoo workers; and, of course, visits from senior citizens in the community who have great tales to tell the young.
- Be proud that you have the chance to be a V.I.P. (Virtually Irrepressible Patriot) of education, and, therefore, of the future of humankind!

Some people believe that we are in the midst of the era when students stopped bringing apples to their teachers and began bringing boxes of Extra Strength Tylenol! Perhaps their perception is true. If so, take a pill — and enjoy teaching!

APPENDIX:

More Bright Ideas

Be not the first by whom the new are tried,
Nor yet the last to lay the old aside.
— *Alexander Pope*

"More Bright Ideas" is a collection of little tips and hints, some of which have been generously donated by colleagues. Although all the ideas may not be new and original, they *all* work! I hope you find at least one idea that you can hardly wait to try!

- **THE FISH BOWL:** Keep every student's name on a folded slip of paper in a bowl or other container so that when you need volunteers, and everyone wants the job, you can choose fairly. Once you have drawn a name from the bowl, place the slip elsewhere until all students' names have been drawn.
- **THE SUPPLY LIBRARY:** Establish a box of frequently misplaced or used-up supplies such as pencils, glue, erasers and scissors. You can collect a small sum from each student, ask for donations, or obtain supplies from the office, perhaps — budgets are tight these days! — to get this library started. Then, if students need to borrow items, they sign them out (name, date, item) and give their requests to the supply librarian, a student chosen on merit or by volunteering. Once a week the librarian checks up on items not returned; these must be paid for or replaced by the student before he or she can borrow again. Instituting such a system eliminates the problem of students always using your materials and teaches responsibility.
- **WALL WRITING:** Attach a very large piece of paper (at least 1 m sq.) to one area of the wall and allow students to write anything they want on it. Encourage expression of feelings (e.g., "I am mad!"), little notes to one another, ("Ann, thanks for your help in math"), or even silly diagrams. Once the paper is totally filled, (it somehow becomes more fun the fuller it gets),

exchange it for a clean sheet, and start wallpapering a boring part of your room with the full sheet! The activity is great for Junior High.

- **BEHAVIOR STICKS:** (thanks to Marilyn Reynolds) In a class where behavior can be a concern, give each student a set number of popsicle sticks, with his/her name written on them at the beginning of each day. If the student misbehaves, ask for a stick. At the end of the day, reinforcements are earned according to how many sticks remain.

- **EASY GROUPING:** To get students who sit in desks into groups easily and quickly, arrange your seating plan so that the four members of a group sit in a square. At an established signal from you, each student lifts and turns his or her desk inward, so that all four are facing.

In a class it's easiest if there are even numbers, so that it works like this.

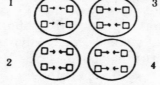

However, if there is another row, those students can leave their desks and move to a different area altogether (e.g., a table). Students return to their original positions in the same manner, on cue. It's possible to go from a class setting to a group setting in less than 30 seconds and with a minimum of noise with this routine. Challenging the students to be faster than last time helps too.

- **GIVE OF YOURSELF:** Teachers are often at a loss as to what small gifts they can give their students at Christmas, or birthdays, or even as prizes. Try giving your time — a coupon with 10 min of teacher time. This can be traded in by the student whenever he/she wants some of your individual time for tutoring, talking or just for company. The amount of time given varies according to the prize. I have known students to save their coupons until they have enough to go for lunch, for example.

126

- **THE TIME-IS-MONEY TREE:** Bring a tree branch to school (you can spray paint it if you wish), and stand it up in a lump of clay. Attach to it, using paper clips as hooks, folded pieces of paper with different amounts of time on each (e.g., 2 min; 5 min). Any time you wish to reinforce a behavior, let a student pick a paper, and gain the amount of free time the paper suggests. Just make it clear that the free time cannot be used during important teaching or seat work. But students can save their times — to a maximum of 15 min (or whatever is good for you). They love the anticipation and luck associated with this ordinarily normal practice of granting free time!

- **THE THEME TREE:** Decorate a tree branch (as in previous example) according to your current theme or to the seasonal holidays. For example, if you are using a science fiction theme in Language Arts, hang such things as foil stars, planets, and pictures of rocket ships and astronauts from the branches. At Halloween, decorate your tree with ghosts, bats and the like; at Christmas, use candy canes, paper-wrapped candies, Christmas crackers, etc. Or, if you focus on birthdays (especially good at Kindergarten and Grade 1), hang the name of the birthday child, along with strands of coiled ribbon, cards from others in the class, etc. This tree can become a focal point in your classroom.

- **FREE-TIME FILE:** Some students are always finished their work before others, so before ever beginning a task, students should be told specifically what they are to do when finished; their options should be written on a section of board reserved for this purpose. One item on my list of free-time activities (which changes according to what needs to be done) is use of the Free-Time File. This file-folder box, which keeps pages neater than a file folder itself, can be painted a bright color in art class and filled with fun worksheets such as unique coloring designs and crosswords. If you have access to the computer program that makes crosswords and word searches, make up some using the students' own names — they love these! You can also provide mazes, funny short stories or comic/cartoon books, and teen/rock star magazines (wrestling magazines are currently popular at Junior High).

  You may wish to have two separate boxes: one for papers, one for reading materials. Keep the boxes up-to-date by constantly adding new materials. Students generally are very good about returning such resources and, of course, the fun pages are theirs to keep. I rely heavily on ideas from teachers' magazines and stores for these files.

- **THE HELPER SYSTEM:** Students who feel they have a skill in a particular area can be encouraged to fill in an application form explaining their skill, their available time for tutoring, (recess, noons, etc.) and what age level they would like to assist. Applications can be made available to all teachers, secretaries, and custodians (some students really want to help a custodian once informed that this is an option). The appropriate adult interviews the student and "hires" him or her, if desired. The services are voluntary, but often little tokens of appreciation are exchanged. This practice often develops into a buddy tutorial system between young and older students.

- **THE WHITE ELEPHANT EXCHANGE:** Students can bring to school any books, unbroken toys, games, and so on, of which they have grown tired, and, at a predesignated time, can barter with one another and exchange. (Be sure to get parents' permission first.) This activity is an excellent technique for teaching the concept of barter (Social Studies), and it promotes communication and socialization skills.

- **THE INDIVIDUAL BOOK:** Students save all of their writing (or as much as possible) throughout the year. In June each student makes a cover and title page, and you coil all their pages of writing into a book for them. What a feeling of accomplishment for students of any age to see their work bound! (Coilers are available in most school resource centres if your school doesn't have one.)

- **THE BEAN JAR:** On your desk keep a small jar or graduated cylinder into which you drop a kidney bean each time you see a behavior you like. Remember to comment specifically on the behavior at the same time, too. When the beans reach a predetermined level, the class may choose one of a variety of rewards such as free time, an extra gym class, a game, or a film. (thanks to Donna Zingle)

There are more bright ideas around than any teacher can ever use. The key is to find the ones that work for you. Since the ideas described in this section have all been used successfully by teachers, that means they are useful and their merits are real! Use them to help you to teach with pizzazz and zeal!

128

Index